Encyclopedia of Top Secret Ways To Defeat "Old Age"

by Frank W. Cawood and Janice McCall Failes

FC&A Publishing
103 Clover Green
Peachtree City, Georgia 30269

First edition. Printed and bound by the Banta Company. Cover design by Debbie Williams.

ISBN # 0-915099-15-2

Acknowledgements

To Linda Sciullo, for pulling all the pieces and people together, while providing encouragement and friendship.

To Betty Whitefield, Wanda Jennings, Jan Ulery, and Gayle Cawood for their untiring proofreading and corrections.

To the entire staff of FC&A, whose hard work enabled us to publish this book.

To B., my best friend, greatest critic and unending source of confidence and faith. Thanks.

To Gayle, Benjamin and Joseph, for your love and support.

To the many people who have touched our lives and inspired us to write this book by their example of growing old gracefully.

Do not cast me off in the time of old age,
Forsake me not when my strength is spent.

Psalms 71:9

And therefore if a man lives many years,
let him enjoy all of them.

Eccelesiates 11:8

Table of Contents

How To Stay In Good Health
As You Grow Older

Do not resent growing old:
Many are denied the privilege.
                                    J.C. Daisley

Have you ever wondered why some people are almost never sick? — why one person may look and feel ten or twenty years younger than his age, while another person the same age may look and feel much older than his age? Many of these youthful people know some of the top secret ways to defeat "old age" that we reveal in this book.

In this <u>Encyclopedia</u> <u>of</u> <u>Top</u> <u>Secret</u> <u>Ways</u> <u>to</u> <u>Defeat</u> "<u>Old</u> <u>Age</u>", we have gathered the best remedies and tips to help ward off many diseases and problems associated with growing older. Many of these suggestions have been taken directly from the best and most up-to-date medical journals. Yet, some of the remedies have worked for generations. Together, all of these tips form an excellent resource to help you defeat the "old age mentality" that there isn't anything you can do to stay healthy as you grow older.

Each person's general health is affected by four factors — body, mind, emotions and spirit. Together, these areas encompass a complete and whole person. If one area is neglected, the person as a whole is not well or complete. When discussing how aging affects us, we should consider the whole person, not just the physical ways the body is changing.

As our bodies are changing and feeling the effects of the years, our spirits often are soaring after we have climbed so many steps during our lifetimes and passed beyond the demands of things like child rearing and "keeping up with the Jones". But now, frustration often results because our spirit is willing... but our bodies are not always able to do what we want them to. Learning to live with the differences in what we want to do and what our bodies can do, eases many emotional problems that can cripple us as we get older. In this book you'll find many ways to grow old

9

gracefully and to continue to enjoy life.

What Causes Aging? — What causes us to age and can we extend our lives are questions that have been asked since Adam and Eve walked out of the Garden of Eden. Several theories on aging are being tested and discussed around the world, but so far, not one theory has been proven.

The main theories about the causes of aging are the "time-table theory" or the "damage theory". The "time-table theory" postulates that our cells are genetically programmed to grow, develop and die in a certain length of time. Dr. W. Donner Denckla believes that there is a single hormone that starts working in our bodies to counteract the activities of healthy cells. He believes that as we grow older, we don't have a shortage of our immune system cells or cardiovascular cells, but that this "death hormone" just stops them from functioning properly. Denckla believes that the thyroid gland produces this hormone, and he is working on isolating it. He believes that if he can find the "death hormone" scientists could develop a drug to stop its action.

The damage theory states that something external damages our cells, causing them to age. Things like radiation, or chemicals in the environment and in our food have been blamed for damaging our cells and causing aging.

As we grow older, our bodies change. At one time, many doctors believed that we reach a plateau in our health, and then suddenly start to decline. Now most researchers believe that aging changes are very gradual and that different parts of our body can age at different rates. For example, a 65 year old man may have the same lung capacity as a 50 year old man, but his kidneys may function as if they are 80 years old.

Because of the body's changes, prescription drugs and some diseases may affect older people differently than younger people. Scientists are just starting to measure and define these age related differences. As the differences are explored, more accurate medical tests and better health care for the elderly will develop.

Extending Life: The Fantasies

Life expectancy, the number of years the average person will live, has steadily increased. Because of improved sanitation, better nutrition, improved control of disease, and better medical care, the average American can now expect to live to be 74.1 years. (based on figures released by the U.S. Department of Health and Human Services). The average woman will live to 77.9 years, while the average man will live to 70.3 years. Many medical researchers believe much of the difference between the two sexes can be directly attributed to smoking. Since more men have smoked, fewer will live longer. Unfortunately, as more women have taken up smoking in recent years, their life expectancy is shortened.

Here are a number of supposed anti-aging remedies. Not one of these has yet been medically proven to lengthen human life.

>DHEA (dehydroepiandrosterone) is a steroid hormone produced by the adrenal glands near the kidneys. In tests on animals DHEA seems to fight cancer, diabetes, obesity and anemia, as well as slow down the aging process. DHEA was available in oral doses in health food stores until the U.S. Food and Drug Administration (FDA) banned it in 1985. DHEA has never been tested in people, and the DHEA sold in health food stores was not produced in government inspected laboratories. Researchers feel there may be some anti-aging benefits from taking DHEA, but that present evidence is inconclusive.

>There is a theory that aging is caused by damage to antioxidants in our cells. Antioxidants are compounds that fight "free radicals". Free radicals are chemicals that are produced in all oxygen-using animals. Free radicals bounce around in our bodies causing damage to cells and molecules. Some researchers think that our bodies produce enough natural antioxidants to fight the free radicals. Others believe that extra supplements of antioxidants are beneficial.

Common antioxidants are the synthetic compound BHT (butylated hydroxy-toluene), vitamins A, C and E, minerals selenium and zinc, and SOD (superoxide dismutase) which is naturally produced in the body.

>There are no vitamins that have been proven to stop the aging process, although proper vitamin intake not greatly exceeding the recommended daily amounts helps the body resist many problems associated with aging. We believe that a healthy diet will increase the chances of living an extended life span. Here are several possible, **but unproven**, ways of slowing down the aging

process with vitamins.

— Vitamin B-15. Russian scientists claim a substance called B-15 (calcium pangamate), which is not accepted as a true vitamin, will slow down the aging process. They say it will retard aging and help prevent or cure heart disease, diabetes, gangrene, high blood pressure, schizophrenia, cirrhosis, hepatitis, and jaundice.

— Vitamin C supplements may help fight aging by strengthening the body's immune system, but very large doses may do more harm than good.

— Vitamin D. Researchers at the University of Michigan claim Vitamin D deficiency causes hearing loss by causing small blood vessels in the ears to deteriorate. They say that vitamin D supplements often help hearing loss and may even prevent deafness.

— Vitamin E. Some nutritionists believe vitamin E can help strengthen the body's immune system and protect it from aging.

>Triosephosphate isomerase (TPI) is an enzyme that researchers claim will reverse the affects of aging. Dr. Robert Gracy at the North Texas State University says TPI stimulates the white blood cells to fight infection, and that it can extend your life by ten years.

>Dr. Roy Walford, professor of immunology and pathology at UCLA School of Medicine, claims that having a restricted diet is the way to long life. Dr. Walford says the key is undernourishment, not malnourishment. He believes that the daily diet should be cut to 1,500 calories a day while maintaining a good intake of all essential vitamins, fatty acids, amino acids and minerals. Although this theory has worked in animal research, it has not been proven in people.

>Russian scientists claim that they have stopped aging by injecting people with a human placenta serum. In 17 years of the study, the participants' blood pressure has returned to normal, they have continued with their regular diets and activities, their sexual functioning has remained normal, and their memories and agility have improved, the researchers claim.

>Dr. Barnet Rosenberg, of Michigan State University is experimenting with extending life by lowering body temperature. According to his animal studies, lowering the body's temperature

12

just two degrees, could extend our life expectancy. Lowering body temperatures actually doubled the life span of rats in his tests.

>Doctors in Russia and Sweden have linked an active sex life to a longer life. There also seems to be a direct correlation between being sexually active and avoiding disease, the Russian doctors claim.

>A wide variety of drugs in the United States and around the world have been promoted as anti-aging "miracles". Here are a few of them:

— Dr. Arthur C. Walsh, of the University of Pittsburgh, combats senility with anticoagulants, "blood thinners", drugs that prevent the formation of blood clots.

— Gerovital® or GH3. This Romanian drug used to treat depression, rheumatoid arthritis and high blood pressure may also have anti-aging properties. It has been tested in Romania since 1949. It was the subject of a controversial losing battle with the U.S. Food and Drug Administration (FDA) in the 1970's.

— Centrophenoxine. This drug is used in West Germany and throughout Europe to combat senility and increase the life span.

>Dr. Carl Pfeiffer claims "brewer's yeast is a good source of the nucleic acids that are the key to staying young."

>Freezing "T-cells", white blood cells, from a healthy, young person and then injecting them back into the same person about 30 years later will boost our immune system and lengthen our lives, according to Dr. Takashi Makinodan. Makinodan is director of Geriatric Research at the Veterans Administration's Wadsworth Hospital in Los Angeles. T-cells are special white blood cells that fight disease, bacteria, germs and viruses. This therapy has only been tested on animals.

Finally, the tips reported in this book are not guaranteed to succeed with everyone. As we wrote this book, we realized that we could not pass judgment on the effectiveness of most secrets that we discovered. Some of these may work for you but not for other people. Some may work for other people but not for you. Many of the tips reported in this book may be controversial or unproven by controlled scientific studies. We've reported them because there is some evidence that they have worked for some people. In doing this, we have attempted to separate fact from fiction and to give special attention to ways to prevent many problems associated with aging which have been confirmed by scientific research. We have attempted, wherever possible, to verify the accuracy of information reported in this book. Nevertheless, since these are reports of the research of other people, we cannot guarantee their safety or effectiveness.

Because of the possibility of errors in reporting the research of others, and because medical science is such a rapidly expanding field with new developments being reported each day, we ask that you consult carefully with your own physician before trying any of the ways to defeat "old age" listed in this book.

It can be dangerous to rely on self-treatment or home remedies and neglect proven medical treaments, such as surgery in cases of cancer. A good physician is the best judge of what sort of medical treatment may be needed for certain diseases. It's good to choose a physician who is open-minded about safe, natural methods of prevention and treatment of problems related to growing old.

Research may one day find a medical treatment to greatly lengthen our lives. But for now, the best ways to naturally combat the symptoms of aging are to eat moderate amounts of healthy food, exercise, take good care of our bodies, plan for the future and enjoy life to the fullest.

In the pages ahead we reveal hundreds of little known ways to fight many diseases and conditions that increase as we get older. Even though the "fountain of youth" still hasn't been discovered, there are many things we can do to avoid or minimize everything from Alzheimer's disease to wrinkles and stay in good health as we grow old gracefully.

Aging Symptoms

•A deficiency of the mineral selenium may result in symptoms of premature aging. Adults need 50 - 200 mcg. of selenium daily.

•Aging may be a reason for taking supplemental thiamine. Changes in taste, financial changes which alter dietary intake, and normal changes in the intestinal lining with aging can result in a decrease of thiamine levels. The Recommended Daily Allowance (RDA) of the thiamine (also known as vitamin B1) is 1.2-1.5 mg. for adult males and 1.0-1.1 for adult females.

•Vitamin E supplements may help reduce the rate of aging according to recent studies. Adult males require 12-15 I.U.'s of vitamin E daily, while adult females need 12 I.U.'s, according to the Recommended Daily Dietary Allowance (RDA) set by the U.S. Government Dept. of Health and Social Services.

Alcoholism

•Alcoholism occurs when people drink alcohol regularly to the extent that it affects their health. Some people can become alcoholics without ever being noticeably drunk, but other alcoholics may frequently go on binges where they drink so much that they pass out.

•Alcoholism is a disease of the spirit, will, mind and body. The first step towards control of the illness is a determination on the part of the alcoholic that he wants to be cured and is willing to endure the physical hardships of withdrawal from alcohol. Once that decision is made, the best procedure is to get help by withdrawing from alcohol in a hospital where physical barriers prevent the alcoholic from having second thoughts and once again returning to alcohol.

>After a few weeks, the recovering alcoholic, when he's released, will be greatly helped by joining a group like Alcoholics Anonymous. At AA, the alcoholic and his family can receive support from a "higher power" and from other people who have experienced victory with their alcoholism.

>Also of high value in helping the alcoholic recover are encouraging support from family and hard work, which includes physical labor in an atmosphere free of alcohol and other addictive substances such as cigarette smoking. Most alcoholics are also

addicted to nicotine. Successfully giving up smoking can help reinforce the decision to give up alcohol. Aerobic exercise, like jogging, walking or hard physical labor, is a great help in preventing the return to alcohol.

>Avoiding sugar and eating regular meals of vitamin rich foods can help the body resist imbalances in blood sugar levels which may cause recovered alcoholics to crave alcohol.

>Supplements of vitamins, especially B vitamins, help correct some of the physical imbalances caused by alcoholism. Large doses (500 mg.) of niacin taken at mealtimes under a doctor's supervision may help reduce the craving for alcohol.

•All efforts to treat alcoholism should be carried on with the support of competent physicians, concerned relatives, friends and pastoral care.

Alzheimer's Disease

•It is estimated that over 2.5 million Americans, mostly elderly, suffer from some form of Alzheimer's disease, a serious progressive deterioration of the brain. Alzheimer's victims can live as long as ten years but death normally occurs within a few months. It is difficult to diagnose. Furthermore, as memory degenerates and confusion takes over, care of an Alzheimer's patient may become difficult.

•No one knows the cause of Alzheimer's disease, but according to Dr. Robert Friedland of the National Institute on Aging, the disease attacks the brain cells. Many physicians suspect a slow-acting virus or viral particle which attacks the brain is the cause.

•Memory loss is one of the chief symptoms of Alzheimer's disease, but an accurate diagnosis should be made by a competent physician since some memory loss is normal as people age. A loss of the ability to solve problems, confusion, irritability, lack of ability to concentrate or learn new things, depression, changes in personality, wandering, delusions, loss of bladder and bowel control, loss of ability to talk and a reduction in the ability to complete the everyday tasks of living are also associated with Alzheimer's disease.

Memory loss in Alzheimer's patients is different than memory loss in other adults. Lisa P. Gwyther, who wrote the book, Care of Alzheimer's Patients: A Manual for Nursing Home Staff, explains that many adults forget things. A normal adult will forget part of an event but the Alzheimer's victim will forget the whole event, says Gwyther. A normal adult will eventually remember what they forgot. They will feel guilty because they forgot something. A person with Alzheimer's will forget the event, never remember it in the future and won't even realize that they have forgotten anything, she explains. Memory loss is progressive and continues to get worse, according to Gwyther.

•Lecithin supplements may help reduce the risk of developing Alzheimer's. Researchers have found that patients with Alzheimer's disease have a deficiency of acetylcholine in their brain tissue. Acetylcholine is a natural substance that helps transmit nerve reactions in the brain. However, science does not currently know how to replace the lost acetylcholine. Lecithin, a substance extracted from egg yolks, soybeans and other high-fat foods, is thought to be important in replacing acetylcholine. The vitamin choline forms part of the nervous system transmitter acetylcholine and is naturally found in lecithin, soybeans, eggs, fish, liver, wheat germ, green vegetables, peanuts, brewer's yeast, and sunflower seeds.

Memory loss improved in middle-aged people after taking lecithin supplements in a West German study. In a study in England, the progress of Alzheimer's disease was slowed down when lecithin was taken for at least six months. Lipton® soup may capitalize on these new studies. They are thinking about selling a new "healthy" soup containing a high percentage of pure lecithin.

•Low levels of vitamin B12 (cobalamin) and zinc were found in people with Alzheimer's disease in a study published in the Journal of Orthomolecular Psychiatry. The research conducted in The Netherlands showed that if Alzheimer's is recognized at an early stage, treatment with vitamin B12 and zinc may help restore memory. Liver, meat, milk, dairy products, fish and eggs are good sources of vitamin B12. Zinc is found naturally in liver, seafood, dairy products, meat, eggs and whole-grain products.

•Loss of estrogen may play a part in the development of Alzheimer's in postmenopausal women, according to Dr. Bruce

McEwen of Rockefeller University. Dr. McEwen found that women with Alzheimer's had lower estrogen levels than their healthy counterparts, reports an article in the Saturday Evening Post. He also discovered that estrogen, a natural hormone, seems to have an effect on the brain cells that is opposite to the effect of Alzheimer's disease. Alzheimer's causes the nerve cells to degenerate, while estrogen enables them to thrive. Initial tests are being conducted on the use of estrogen in female Alzheimer's patients. The final role of estrogen supplements in treating Alzheimer's is not known.

•According to a recent study by Stuart Shalat of Harvard University, you can get Alzheimer's disease from the air you breathe. The study linked cigarette smoking to an increased occurrence of Alzheimer's disease. Based on the study results, people who smoked more than one pack of cigarettes per day were four times as likely to develop Alzheimer's disease as non-smokers.

•Autopsies of Alzheimer's victims have revealed higher than normal levels of aluminum in brain tissue. Theoretically, preventing the accumulation of aluminum in elderly people may slow or prevent the development of the disease. Researchers are evaluating the role of aluminum in the development of Alzheimer's (New England Journal of Medicine) but scientific studies are not yet completed to prove or disprove this theory. If you want to be cautious and avoid possible exposure to aluminum, the University of California, Berkeley Wellness Letter (Vol. 3 Issue 1) suggests:

>Avoid foods containing aluminum.

>Do not cook apples, tomatoes or sauerkraut in aluminum pots because these highly acidic foods leach out the aluminum from the cook ware.

>Don't buy or drink carbonated beverages from aluminum cans.

>Do not store acidic or salty foods in aluminum foil.

>Drink three glasses of skim milk per day to help the body displace aluminum.

>Take fluoride supplements which may prevent the accumulation of aluminum in the brain.

>Do not use antacids that contain aluminum.

>Avoid areas with known acid rain. Dr. Daniel Peter Perl

from the Mount Sinai Hospital in New York suggests that acid rain "leaches aluminum out of the soil into our drinking water". He believes that acid rain may be dangerously increasing our exposure to aluminum.

•Columbia University's Health and Nutrition Newsletter (3:2) suggests several ways to help live with an Alzheimer's victim:

>If Alzheimer's is suspected, be sure to have the victim examined by a doctor. Several serious but treatable diseases can cause memory loss and confusion that are often attributed to Alzheimer's disease. Strokes, brain tumors, prescription drugs, heart attacks, chronic insomnia, heart failure, irregular heart rhythms, kidney or liver failure, high or low blood sugar, thyroid problems, lung disease, dehydration and nutritional deficiencies can cause symptoms similar to Alzheimer's disease.

>Keep surroundings familiar to the patient. Don't move furniture or change the home in a drastic way. Try to provide a consistent environment for the person. Keep an Alzheimer's patient in his community since traveling can be very disconcerting.

>Don't allow the victim to wander away from home. Alzheimer's victims should wear an I.D. bracelet or chain that identifies them as an Alzheimer's patient and gives their home address and phone number.

>If just minor memory loss has occurred, help the person by making lists and setting alarm clocks for times to take drugs or eat. As the memory loss progresses, you may need to take the person to the bathroom at certain intervals since he may not remember to go on his own. A high-fiber diet and drinking lots of fluids should help maintain regularity.

>Encourage the person to eat a healthful, balanced diet and do not allow alcoholic beverages. Alzheimer's victims may reject some important foods, but try to creatively provide good nutrition for them. Research has linked some nutritional deficiencies to Alzheimer's disease, but conclusive evidence is not yet available. Therefore, maintaining a well-balanced diet is extremely important.

>You may need to remind the victim to brush his teeth. If the patient is unable to or refuses to brush his teeth, someone should help him or the teeth will quickly deteriorate.

>Help reinforce familiar information. Names of family

members may be forgotten, so keep labeled family pictures around to reinforce the names. Labeling simple tasks that are now difficult may also help the patient. For example, tape "OFF" and "ON" onto light switches.

>Keep new information simple and fresh. Don't expect the person to remember new information. Tell him about it just before the event or activity. Otherwise, it could be forgotten.

>Allow simple decisions. Even though people with Alzheimer's may have a difficult time making decisions, be sure to encourage them. It is easier for them to choose between two options rather than to make an open-ended decision. For example, "Would you like to read or would you like to go for a walk?", is better than "What would you like to do?"

>Concentrate on the skills they have, rather than the skills they have lost. Encourage them to do the things they can do and enjoy doing.

>Provide lots of touching and obvious love. Although Alzheimer's patients don't realize exactly what has happened, they do sense frustration and feel that "something" is wrong. Hugging and touching provide reassurance and aid relaxation.

>Try to keep Alzheimer's victims in good mental spirits and encourage suitable exercise so the body stays as healthy as possible. Walking with or without a walker is great exercise. Even rocking in a chair exercises some muscles and helps to keep blood flowing.

Angina Pectoris

Angina pectoris is chest pain that is caused by heart disease which is more likely to occur as we get older. The amount of angina pain experienced is NOT related to the severity of the heart disease according to a ten-year study by the U.S. Veterans Administration. Therefore, people with only minor angina may be suffering from extensive heart disease.

Severe angina pectoris is often treated with prescription drugs, but the following simple suggestion may help relieve some of the pain. A report in Geriatrics (40: 23) recommends raising the head of your bed by about 10 inches, so that gravity helps take the strain of circulation off your heart.

Cold can worsen angina attacks. In tests, angina attacks can be brought on by placing the hand of an angina patient in a basin of ice water. Angina sufferers should prepare for cold weather or cold situations by dressing warmly and in layers. Protect your face and head especially, since most of your body's heat escapes from the head. You should avoid going out into cold weather and avoid any strenuous activity in the cold.

Men suffering from angina pectoris should try wearing a girdle around the waist, according to Dr. Peter J. Steincrohn. This doctor believes, and has supporting testimonies, that wearing a girdle (often called an abdominal support) helps ease the strain on the heart. Supporting the abdominal muscles helps increase circulation. To ask a man to wear a girdle may sound utterly ridiculous . . . but once most men with angina try it for a week they realize that they are less fatigued and suffer fewer angina attacks, says Dr. Steincrohn. Wearing a girdle that provides support of the "pot belly" seems to be an easy and inexpensive way to reduce angina.

For some angina patients, an aspirin a day can reduce the chance of having a heart attack, the Food and Drug Administration (FDA) says. One aspirin tablet per day can cut heart attacks by 20% for some people who have already had heart attacks to as much as 50% in men who have unstable angina. In patients with unstable angina, an aspirin a day reduced, by about half, the risk of getting a heart attack or of dying of a heart attack. During the three-month study, the risk of having a heart attack was lowered from a 12% chance without aspirin to a 6% chance with aspirin. Aspirin is not a substitute for other preventative therapies for heart attacks, cautions FDA commissioner Frank E. Young, M.D. He advises that patients consult their physicians before starting daily aspirin.

Vitamin E may play a role in helping to reduce angina pain. At the University of British Columbia in Canada, Dr. Terence W. Anderson has done preliminary tests with angina patients taking vitamin E supplements. Although it was a small study including just 15 patients, Dr. Anderson found that angina pain increased when vitamin E supplements were switched to a placebo. The patients did not know their medication was changed. However, every man whose vitamin E was switched asked to be taken out of the study because of an increase in angina pain. Whole-grain products, green vegetables, milk, almonds, peanuts, pecans, soybeans, eggs and meat are good natural sources of vitamin E. Use caution when taking vitamin E because large doses of vitamin E can be dangerous.

The amino acid, L-carnitine, may be useful in treating angina, according to research by Dr. Robert Atkins.

People receiving digitalis or other heart medication should not take calcium ascorbate (a vitamin C formulation), since irregular heartbeats may occur.

Here are some general recommendations to help reduce your angina symptoms.

> Lose weight if you are overweight. Be kind to your heart.

> Don't eat too much at one sitting. Overeating or eating at irregular times can disrupt your body and put extra stress on the heart. Rest for at least half an hour after eating.

> Stop smoking. Smoking causes constriction of your arteries which forces your heart to become overworked.

> Exercise. Gradually increasing the amount of exercise you get will help strengthen your heart and arteries and may reduce your angina problems.

> Get proper rest and a good night's sleep. To get a good supply of oxygen and fresh air for the night's sleep, open the windows wide for about 10 minutes, then leave them open about an inch. A stuffy room may inhibit your ability to sleep, according to Dr. Charles Wolfe, Jr. of the Sleep Disorder Center in Chicago.

Appetite — Loss Of

In recent studies, zinc supplements were quite successful in helping people regain their appetite. Apparently, levels of zinc in the body often reach very low levels in crash dieting, and because of the loss of this mineral, people may lose their senses of smell and taste and find that food is unappetizing. Zinc supplements help people to regain their senses of taste and smell and to enjoy eating once again. The Recommended Daily Allowance for zinc is 15 milligrams per day for adults.

In addition to zinc, other vitamin and mineral supplements may be helpful in treating loss of appetite, because vitamins and minerals have a general stimulating effect on tne entire body, including the appetite. In some cases, loss of appetite may be caused by an overdose of calcium or a deficiency of thiamine (vitamin B1), pantothenic acid (vitamin B5), vitamin B12, biotin, phosphorus or zinc.

Loss of appetite is also a common side effect of many prescription drugs, including diuretics (blood pressure lowering drugs), tranquilizers, antidepressants, sleeping aids, anti-inflammatory drugs, and antihistamines.

Arthritis

Arthritis strikes the young and the old, but osteoarthritis is more like to occur as we age.

Usually doctors will recommend rest, an exercise program and thermal (heat) treatments to relieve arthritis naturally. Patients also are reminded to eat a well-balanced diet, maintain good posture and follow all the therapy prescribed by the doctor.

Rest — Especially during flare-ups, plenty of rest should be taken. People with arthritis should stop activities that cause severe pain, and they should never become completely exhausted. Tiredness and severe fatigue often contribute to arthritis, and naps may become part of the daily routine. A balance between rest and activity is needed to prevent inflammation and further damage to affected joints.

Exercise — A proper balance of rest and exercise helps to control arthritis. Exercise is needed to keep joints flexible, restore freedom of movement, improve circulation, and increase mobility. Specific exercise programs often are required to keep muscles and tendons strong and healthy, preventing further stress on joints.

Each person should consult a physician and often a physical therapist about an individual exercise program based on his or her needs. Different joints require different types and amounts of exercise to maintain the full range of motion. Isometric exercises are often advised. Isometrics are exercises that involve muscle contractions while the joints remain in place, like squeezing the hand against a fixed object.

Good general exercises are walking, hiking, swimming and bicycling. Strenuous sports should be avoided. All exercise should be preceded by warm-ups to relax the muscles and prevent injuries.

Movements should be slow and gentle, never jarring the joints. The popular exercise motto "no pain, no gain" is NOT true for people who have arthritis. Arthritis sufferers should NEVER exercise to, or beyond, the point of pain.

Regular, doctor-approved exercise should be done at least 15 minutes a day, 5 to 7 days a week. During flare-ups when joints are very swollen, red and tender to the touch, exercises should be alternated with periods of rest, or exercising should be discontinued.

Exercising in water, known as hydrotherapy, sometimes is recommended because water helps support the joints during exercising. This allows the person to exercise all major muscle groups without putting stress on the affected joints. The Arthritis Foundation, in cooperation with the YMCA's and YWCA's, offers "exercising in the water" or "warm water" programs especially for sensitive joints.

Weight Control — Maintain your ideal weight. Obesity places additional strain on inflamed joints. A weight reduction diet may be recommended by your doctor to reduce excess pressure on the joints.

Thermal Therapy — Heat is an excellent way to relieve pain, relax muscles, increase joint mobility and decrease joint and tissue inflammation. A hot shower or bath in the morning can loosen stiffness which invades joints during sleep or limber up stiff joints before exercising.

There are numerous ways to obtain heat such as baths, showers, hot packs and compresses, hot water bottles, 250-watt reflector heat lamps, electric pads, whirlpools, hot springs, saunas and warm paraffin wax treatments. Moist heat is usually preferable to dry heat. Sustaining comfortable heat levels for a longer period of time is better than applying heat that is too hot. Be careful to ensure that skin is protected from burns. Don't use the heat for more than twenty minutes at a time because after that heat loses its effectiveness. Never use a hair dryer, sun lamp, tanning booth or ultraviolet light to provide heat.

You can make excellent hot packs by soaking towels in hot water, then covering them with plastic wrap to hold the heat for as long as possible.

Hot wax treatments use melted paraffin applied to the affected joints. The best way to melt the paraffin is in an electric deep fat fryer, but the top of a double boiler can also be used on an electric burner. Do not use a gas burner because the flame may ignite fumes from the paraffin. Wax maintains the heat on your body for long periods of time, but it can be messy or dangerous and should not be used if there are open cuts. If you and your doctor think that you are capable of handling paraffin wax, take precautions. Use a candy thermometer and don't heat the paraffin above 110° F. Keep a fire extinguisher handy and practice putting a lid on the double boiler with a long handled fork in case the paraffin catches on fire. Wax is easiest to use on small joints such as the hands, wrists or feet.

Electric blankets are an excellent source of heat for relieving the stiffness of arthritis. An electric blanket provides consistent, even heat without the bulk of heavy comforters or quilts. Heavy blankets can put too much strain on the feet and joints and cause an arthritis flare-up. Hot water bottles lose their heat too quickly, and heating pads can burn the skin, so an electric blanket may be the best remedy for sore joints.

Another way to sleep with warm, moist heat is by using a heated water bed. Many people find that the warmth of the water combined with the support of the "flexible" water mattresses helps soothe their arthritis flare-ups.

Some people claim sleeping in a sleeping bag reduces their morning stiffness. No one is exactly sure why a sleeping bag helps, but it is worth a try if morning stiffness is a problem.

Use hot or cold treatments to help reduce pain and swelling. Some people find heat works best for them, whereas other people experience the most relief from cold. Many prefer alternating between hot and cold treatments.

Cold therapy may reduce the pain. Arthritis symptoms sometimes respond well to cold treatments with compresses or ice packs which can reduce inflammation. The Journal of the American Medical Association (JAMA 246: 317) reports that ice cube therapy provided relief for arthritics at Oregon University. For twenty minutes, three times each day, six ice cubes in plastic bags were placed just above and just below the knees of arthritic patients. Even though the cold therapy took a little while to get used to, each patient decided to continued with the ice cube treatment because of the great relief it provided.

To prevent harming the skin by directly applying ice, some doctors recommend making an ice pack from a towel. Soak a small towel in water, then wring it out. Place the towel on a sheet of aluminum foil in a freezer to keep it from sticking to the freezer. When ice crystals appear, you can use the towel. Be sure to use it before it is completely frozen. This "ice pack" will conform to your joints and provide a great cold treatment.

Joint Protection — Many people can relieve symptoms by learning to use joints carefully and relieving extra pressure on inflamed areas. Canes, walkers and crutches can reduce the amount of body weight placed on joints. Splints or braces may be used to hold joints in position and protect them. Good posture can protect joints and prevent further damage.

Shoes should be purchased with extra care because the feet support the body's weight. High heels should be avoided. They don't distribute body weight evenly, and they cause people to walk awkwardly. Low-heeled shoes that provide solid support, lots of room for the toes to move, a snug heel and cushioning make it easier to walk with correct posture and protect the joints.

Perform everyday activities in a way that will least likely affect the arthritis joints. For example, rather than lifting large items, slide them across the floor.

Use purses or pocketbooks with shoulder straps rather than carrying all the weight with the fingers and wrist. Push suitcases on wheels rather than carrying them. When facing everyday situations, consider your joints and how you can protect them from unnecessary stress and further damage.

Diet and Nutrition — Nutrition plays an important role in preventing many illnesses, but a specific diet has never been proven to control any form of arthritis except gout. Arthritis sufferers should eat a well-balanced diet to consume the government- recommended daily allowance (RDA's) of vitamins and minerals to maintain stamina and health.

Of course, obesity places more strain on inflamed joints. A weight reduction diet may be recommended by doctors to reduce pressure on the joints.

Some people, including a number of physicians, claim that a diet, largely composed of unsalted rice and fish that excludes dairy products, wheat, meat and all processed foods, is helpful for some cases of arthritis, particularly rheumatoid arthritis. No one has made controlled studies on this diet, but proponents of the diet have numerous testimonials from people who claim to have been helped by such a diet.

Such a diet theoretically could be helpful to some people even though this is unproven. Researchers recently have discovered anti-inflammatory properties in fish oil. Allergic reactions by some people to certain foods could possibly cause arthritis symptoms. The Arthritis Foundation recommends that if you suspect that a certain food is aggravating your arthritis, try avoiding it for at least two weeks; then see if it makes a difference.

There are two dangers to avoid if you go on such a diet. Rice is a very healthful food, but it's not complete. You need vitamins, minerals and protein from vegetables, fruit and animal protein like fish, plus a small amount of essential fatty acids which can be attained by eating a small amount of vegetable oil each day. Make sure your doctor agrees that any diet you go on is well-balanced. Also, don't put all your faith in an unproven diet and neglect proven treatments.

A diet low in cholesterol, fat and sodium could improve the physical well being of an arthritis victim. Researchers at Wayne State University Medical School in Michigan tested a small group of people with rheumatoid arthritis by placing them on a fat-free diet. Within seven weeks, all of the arthritis had gone into remission. This was only a small test, but a largely fat-free diet, if it is medically supervised, may be worth a try. It might also help people who suffer from obesity, heart disease, high blood pressure, or other degenerative diseases associated with eating excessive amounts of high-fat or high-sodium foods. If this diet, or any other diet, helps a person lose excess weight, it may help relieve arthritis symptoms by reducing strain on weight-bearing joints.

Try eliminating some foods from your diet. Some cases of arthritis are caused by allergies according to the medical journal Arthritis and Rheumatism (29:220). A recent case involved a 52-year old woman who displayed symptoms of rheumatoid arthritis only when she drank or consumed milk. To prove the allergy theory, the doctors gave her tablets that she thought were medication on several different occasions. Sometimes the tablets contained a useless substance and sometimes they actually contained powered milk. In each instance, the pain, stiffness, and swelling returned when the woman received the milk product, even though the woman did not know what she had been given. This case and similiar cases provide a medical basis for considering allergies in cases of arthritis. If a food allergy is suspected, a rotation diet may help.

If you suspect that a certain food is causing your problems, try keeping food and arthritis charts for about two months. On one chart keep track of everything you eat and drink each day. On the other chart, record all of your arthritis symptoms, when they occurred, what joints were affected, how long they lasted and how severe they were. At the end of two months, see if you can notice any correlations between the two charts. Then try to eliminate any suspect foods from your diet. Continue working on both diaries and note any changes in your arthritis.

Avoiding Quack Cures — Since arthritis is a "flare-up" kind of disease, many people will attribute sudden relief to the latest thing they have taken or tried. It is important to remember that, so far, no general medical cure exists for arthritis.

Remissions have caused people to claim that everything from copper bracelets to pineapples can cure arthritis. For every dollar spent in arthritis research, $25.00 will be spent on expensive, unproven remedies.

Strange tales of "how I cured my arthritis" are often caused by the "placebo effect". A "placebo" is a harmless substance given to a patient. The patient is told that it will cure her disease — and because the patient really wants to be cured, or believes that she will be cured, it works!

The Arthritis Foundation used to call all "cures" that were not medically accepted "quack" cures. But now the Arthritis Foundation is being more cautious and refers to them as "unproven" remedies. These "cures" have not been medically proven to cure arthritis and many of them can even be very harmful. But since cures for other diseases have been found in unusual places, like penicillin from mold, perhaps researchers will discover the long awaited cure for arthritis in an unusual remedy. Until then, unproven cures may be harmful and are not recommended.

"Unproven cures" fall into these four categories: drugs and medications, devices, publicized clinics, and nutrition ideas. To avoid these unproven remedies, arthritis sufferers should be cautious of remedies that contain "secret" ingredients, remedies advertised for all types of arthritis, anything advertised as a "cure" for arthritis, and remedies that are supported only by the testimonials of people but have no valid, controlled medical or scientific research supporting them.

Vitamins and Minerals — Since aspirin causes vitamin C to be eliminated from the body, people taking large doses of aspirin (for arthritis) may benefit from vitamin C supplements.

Menopausal arthritis may be reduced with pyridoxine (vitamin B6) supplements.

Some arthritis sufferers claim that pantothenic acid (vitamin B5) is effective in reducing pain. A number of British physicians think that pantothenic acid supplements can prevent the development of rheumatoid arthritis and even osteoarthritis in many people. Long-term, controlled studies will be necessary to verify this claim.

• Aspirin is still the best single medicine to help relieve the pain and swelling of arthritis. However, to keep the pain under control, high doses of aspirin are often required. Be sure to visit your doctor and remain under his regular care even if he advises a non-prescription product like aspirin. High doses of aspirin can reduce the ability of blood to clot and lead to ringing in the ears and stomach irritation. Always take aspirin with a full glass of water or milk to help reduce stomach upset.

Buffered aspirin, coated aspirin or time-released aspirin may cause fewer side effects than regular aspirin, especially when taken in high doses. Be sure you buy an aspirin product and not acetaminophen. Acetaminophen is the active ingredient in Tylenol®, Datril®, Panadol®, Phenaphen®, and Anacin-3®. It is a good pain-reliever but it will not control the swelling of arthritis as aspirin will. Like aspirin, ibuprofen products (including Advil®, Nuprin®, Medipren®, Motrin®, Rufen®, Trendar® and Haltran®) can control both the pain and swelling of arthritis.

An analog of the active ingredient in aspirin, called salicylate, is found in rub-on creams. For small areas of discomfort using a cream may provide more direct relief. The creams are available over-the-counter as Myoflex® and Aspercreme®. Use them only as directed. If you are allergic to aspirin or if you should not use aspirin because of blood clotting problems, avoid these aspirin/cream products.

• Support from family, friends and doctors can make a big difference in the pain the patient feels, according to a recent study by researchers at Indiana University. People with osteoarthritis felt better after receiving a phone call from their doctor every two weeks for six months, the researchers discovered. Each phone call lasted about ten minutes and included questions about how they were feeling and what things they could do for themselves. After the six months, the patients felt less pain than at the beginning of the study. The researchers concluded that although telephone follow-up from doctors could not cure the arthritis, the calls provided emotional support and information for each arthritis sufferer. The calls seemed to relieve the minds of the patients, and they felt less pain, functioned better each day, and were less depressed about their arthritis.

• Dr. Arnold Fox of the University of California at Irvine claims that an amino acid can reduce pain in about 80 percent of the general population. The amino acid is DLPA, short for DL-phenylalanine, is available in many health food stores and drugstores. Dr. Fox recommends 375 to 400 milligrams of DLPA with each meal to reduce the pain of arthritis. DLPA should not be taken by pregnant women or people with phenylketonuria (PKU). It may also cause an unwanted stimulation of the nervous system. It seems to work by stimulating the body's hormones to block the pain signals from the brain, according to the doctor.

• Fish oil supplements containing omega 3 fatty acids may be helpful in reducing morning stiffness and tender joints associated with rheumatoid arthritis, based on a study at Albany Medical College. However, fish oil capsules may contain too much vitamin A which can be toxic (New England Journal of Medicine 316: 10, 626). Nutritionists are recommending incorporating more fish into your regular diet, by eating fish at least twice a week rather than taking concentrated supplements in capsules or tablets. Salmon, mackerel, tuna, sardines, crab, shrimp, lobster and other shellfish are all high in beneficial omega-3 fatty acids.

• Hypnosis may be useful in treating the symptoms associated with arthritis, according to studies by Barbara Domangue, Ph.D. at Jefferson Medical College in Philadelphia. Hypnosis reduced the patients' pain, distress, anxiety and depression and increased the amount of natural painkiller, beta-endorphin, in their blood levels. Do NOT attempt to hypnotize yourself, self-hypnosis can be extremely dangerous — rely on a professional doctor or therapist.

• Learning to live with arthritis can be difficult. There is no known cure for arthritis. However, many of the discomforts of arthritis can be reduced by taking special care of yourself:

> Learn to manage the stress in your life. Major stressful events have been associated with the development of rheumatoid arthritis according to research by Dr. Fred Kantrowitz of the Harvard Medical School. Doctors are not certain whether a stress-filled event actually causes the arthritis or just makes it noticeable. Studies have shown that nearly 10% of women and 25% of children who develop rheumatoid arthritis have experienced a traumatic event.

> Set reasonable goals for yourself. The time it takes you to complete a project may be a lot longer now than before you had arthritis. Don't place yourself under additional stress by setting unrealistic goals.

> Plan the priorities in your life and work to achieve those. Learn to "conserve your energy" for things that are important to you. Planning events while remembering your needs as an arthritic, can help make the most of special and everyday events.

> Develop a positive attitude. Learn to focus on the things you can do rather than dwelling on the pain and limitations arthritis brings. By remaining socially active and concentrating on other things, you can learn to live with your arthritis. Find ways you can help others. This will not only benefit them but will contribute to your own sense of worth and value.

> Respect your pain. Many times people ignore their pain and continue doing harmful activities. You should learn to use your pain to tell you when to slow down, to quit what you are

doing and to rest. Learn when to quit what you are doing and rest before overexertion and unnecessary soreness set in.

• Learning to use your body properly can help reduce the pain and swelling of arthritic joints. Here are some sensible tips from the Arthritis Foundation that can reduce the strain on your joints:

> Always use the largest possible joint or number of joints for each task. For example, use your whole hand, instead of just your fingers. Carry things carefully. Supporting something with two hands may reduce the strain of carrying an object.

> Strive to obtain good posture while sitting or standing. Good posture will improve the muscles' ability to support the joints and will help prevent deformities from occurring.

> Take advantage of some of the many new products for arthritis sufferers. Wide handles, easy-to-open containers, velcro fasteners, elastic shoelaces, buttoning aids and many other inventions can make your life easier.

> Be efficient and save steps when using your joints. When walking, use the shortest possible route. Get extra phones and use them throughout the house or use a cordless phone that you can move with you. Apply for a handicapped-parking permit. Many people with moderate to severe arthritis are eligible for a handicapped permit.

> Use mechanical devices that will help reduce use of your joints. For example, a remote-control TV, stereo and VCR, including volume control, can save many steps. Put lights on timers to help eliminate the need to turn them off and on. A whistle switcher or sound-activated control could save steps. A push-button phone programmed for your most frequently used numbers can be helpful.

> Make your car as easy to use as possible. Use automatic transmission, power windows, power brakes, power door locks, automatic trunk release and any other options that will reduce your need to move.

> Make living within your home as convenient as possible. Try to live on just one level of your house to avoid climbing stairs. Be creative with where you put things that you use frequently. Don't just keep them where you and others have traditionally placed them. For example, you may decide to put your washer and

dryer near your bedroom to save steps. Develop "work centers" so that everything you need for a task is within easy grasp.

> Reduce the amount of bending you need to do. Keep everyday utensils on the counter or stove top so you don't have to bend down to get them. Even though it may not look as tidy, your kitchen will be easier for you to use and enjoy. Store your most-used items at your body level. Place a chair or stool in front of sinks so you can sit at the sink rather than bending over it.

> Use a bench in your bathtub or shower so you can sit while showering. Install grab bars in your shower or over your tub. To prevent slipping, use adhesive rubber strips on the tub or shower floor rather than rubber mats.

> Make your home safe. Put adhesive rubber strips on stairs. Eliminate scatter rugs or tape them to the floor. Put wires and cables behind furniture where they will be out of the way. Make sure the inside and the outside of your home are well-lit so you can see to avoid any obstacles.

> Use comfortable and practical furniture throughout your house and patio. Firm, supportive chairs will be better for you than plush chairs or sofas that are difficult to get in and out of. You may consider getting a lift-chair that helps raise you to a standing position.

> Choose your clothes carefully. Avoid shirts or dresses that fasten up the back. Women can wear bras with a front closure rather than hooks at the back. Use velcro for fasteners. Wear clothes that will keep you comfortable. Buy shoes that are supportive and fit well. For wearing around the house, tennis shoes might be the most comfortable choice. Shoes do not have to be expensive to be well-made and supportive. Do not wear high heels, or wear only heels that are less than one inch high.

> Reduce or eliminate lifting. Push or slide objects or ask someone else to move large objects. Use as much of your body as possible when pushing so there is less strain on an individual joint. For example, don't use your fingers when you can push with your entire hand and perhaps your shoulder. When it is necessary to lift something, use proper lifting techniques. Always use the legs to do the lifting, and bend from the knees, not from the waist. Concentrate on using your thigh muscles (at the top of your legs) rather than your back muscles. Never twist while

lifting. Keep the object you are lifting as close to your body as possible. Even when you are lifting or carrying everyday items, make them as light as you can. Ladies should consider using a smaller purse, for example. Store food in plastic bags or aluminum foil rather than in heavy cooking dishes.

> Within your home, use a cart to help move items from room to room. A cart can be used to help carry dishes, laundry, cleaning supplies and food.

> When serving large numbers of people, use a "buffet-style" set-up so the guests can help themselves to plates, food and drinks. Using one table will save you many steps back and forth to the kitchen.

> Use an electric can opener and an under-the-counter jar opener. The jar opener will allow you to open all sizes of jars without harming your joints.

> If you need a walker, get one with wheels and auto-stops on it because you can roll it without having to lift it. If you use a cane, an adjustable model allowing you to change the height for each situation might be best. The cane should be used on the side of the body that is least affected by the arthritis.

> Using a typewriter rather than writing with a pen or pencil may be helpful. Many people find that typing doesn't bother their joints as much as holding onto a pen or pencil. Consider using a "light touch" typewriter or home computer. When writing, use a felt-tip pen instead of a ball point pen since the felt-tip pen doesn't require as much pressure.

> If grasping small items like pens and table utensils is difficult, try placing a soft foam curler around the item. This will make it larger and softer to hold. Keep a "jar opener" pad in your purse or pocket. You can use the non-slip rubber pad to open doorknobs or other objects even when you are away from home.

> If getting money out of pay-telephones or vending machines is difficult, try using the eraser-end of a pencil to slide the coin out of the slot and into your hand.

> Keep as active as possible. To avoid stiffness, try not to remain in the same position for more than 20 minutes. Maintain good posture when sitting and standing. A ten-year study in The Lancet showed that moderate activity was better than bed rest for sufferers of rheumatoid arthritis.

> Balance your activity with adequate rest. Interrupt long spells of activity with short breaks. Try to get 10 to 12 hours of sleep per night. Most arthritis sufferers seem to need much sleep.

> Plan your schedule around the times your arthritis is most painful. For example, many people find that they're able to enjoy certain activities more in the afternoon than in the morning because most of their joint stiffness has subsided then.

• Weather and climate have NOT been proven to affect arthritis. If you feel that a warmer or drier climate is more suitable for you, consider a long visit before you make a permanent move. However, there is no medical evidence that the climate cures or improves arthritis.

• Sleep on a firm, comfortable mattress. Some people like a firm water bed that can be heated. One company has just designed a special mattress, made from weaving wool, that has been tested by arthritics and people with back problems. Ninety percent of the people in the mattress test found that the new mattress improved their sleep and reduced their arthritis symptoms. Woolrest® is the brand name of this weaving wool mattress.

• Don't sleep on your stomach. This position can damage the alignment of your neck and back.

• If you suffer from stiff hands in the morning, try wearing gloves to bed. Dr. Frank Schmid, in a study for the Arthritis Foundation, discovered that stretch gloves decreased the amount of swelling, numbness and stiffness in arthritic hands..

• For severe morning stiffness, you may want to set your alarm clock half an hour early. If you take an aspirin about 30 minutes before you want to get out of bed, the aspirin will have time to reduce the swelling and pain. Be sure to sit up and drink a large glass of water when swallowing the aspirin or any other medication to make sure that the aspirin reaches the stomach. Never take a pill while lying down because it could get caught in the throat and possibly eat a hole through your esophagus.

• Beware of "false" arthritis. Self-diagnosis can be harmful. If you suspect that you have arthritis (see symptoms following) be sure to see your doctor. Sometimes people who are experiencing joint pain, inflammation or swelling are really suffering from side effects from their prescription drugs. Several common drugs can cause arthritis-like symptoms including Tagamet® (cimetidine), beta blockers like Inderal® (propranolol) or Lopressor® (metoprolol), oral iron supplements, barbiturates, blood-pressure reducers, sulfa drugs, quinidine, penicillamine, diuretics, amphotericin B and tetracycline. Never stop taking any of your prescription drugs without checking with your doctor first.

• Other drugs may aggravate systemic lupus erythematosus, a form of arthritis known as lupus. Oral contraceptives, Apresoline®, penicillin, tetracycline, some sulfa drugs and several anti-cancer drugs can increase the symptoms of lupus.

• If there is a history of arthritis in your family, you should be aware of the early warning signs of arthritis as described by the Arthritis Foundation. If you notice any of these symptoms, discuss them with your doctor.

> Nagging pain and stiffness in the morning.
> Redness or warmth in a joint.
> Pain or tenderness in one or more joints.
> Not being able to move a joint normally.
> Swelling in one or more joints.
> Pain and stiffness in the neck, lower back, knees or other joints.
> Tingling sensations in the fingertips, hands and feet.
> Unexplained weight loss, fever, weakness or tiredness.

Your doctor will want to know several things before he or she can work out a arthritis-care program for you.

> How long are the flare-ups?
> What joints are affected?
> Is it worse in the morning or later in the day?
> Is there any redness or swelling at the site of the soreness?
> Is there any fever or temperature increase?

Asthma

• Asthmatics should practice methods to relieve stress. Asthma is not a psychological disorder. However, strong emotions like stress, worry and fear can trigger an asthma attack. The emotions don't cause the disease itself, but they can aggravate it. Deep breathing exercises and relaxation techniques may help reduce the severity of an attack.

• Yoga may help. According to a study published in the

British Medical Journal (290:6463), asthmatics who practiced yoga exercises for at least six months suffered fewer asthma attacks. The researchers believe that yoga helps to relax the nervous system, which lowers the intensity and frequency of asthma attacks.

• Vigorous exercise, such as running, or drastic changes in temperature, can trigger an attack. An estimated 85% of asthmatics have symptoms of wheezing after exercise, according to the American Academy of Allergy and Immunology. Exercise that requires hard breathing for long periods of time (like long-distance running) and most activities in cold air should be avoided. Swimming is good exercise for an asthmatic because it provides overall exercise, yet the asthmatic's air passages will not dry out due to lack of moisture.

• Do not eat ice cream or drink extremely cold liquids because your bronchial tubes may be shocked into spasms by the cold.

• Avoid foods containing yellow food dye #5. Between 47,000 and 94,000 asthmatics in the U.S. are affected by this food coloring, known as tartrazine yellow. Many other food additives, like BHA and BHT, may aggravate asthma. To avoid dyes and additives, eat non-processed, natural foods when possible. Wash all fruit and vegetables thoroughly before eating. Unfortunately, this will not remove all the chemicals used during growing and transporting, but washing can remove some of them.

• Asthmatics need to avoid beta-blocking drugs or use them only with extreme caution. Beta-blockers, used to help treat high blood pressure, can constrict the bronchial muscles and cause life-threatening problems for an asthmatic. Beta-blockers are widely prescribed and include: acebutolol (Sectral®), atenolol (Tenormin®), labetalol (Normodyne®), metoprolol (Lopressor®), nadolol (Corgard®), pindolol (Visken®), propranolol (Inderal®), and Timolol (Blocadren®). Be sure you and your doctor have thoroughly considered both your asthma and your blood pressure problems. Do not stop taking any medication without your physician's approval.

• Timolol (Timoptic®) eye drops, used to treat glaucoma and pressure in the eye, have been associated with at least five deaths of asthmatics. Timoptic® is applied directly to the eye and is available only by prescription. Notify your eye doctor if you have asthma and are taking this medication.

• Penicillin, aspirin and many other anti-inflammatory drugs can cause severe asthma attacks. Some of these drugs are known as NSAIDs (Non-Steroidal Anti-Inflammatory Drugs). NSAIDs are commonly used to help treat arthritis, menstrual cramps and general pain. Ibuprofen is a NSAID that is available without prescription as Advil®, Haltran®, Medipren®, Nuprin®, Trendar® and several other brands. It is also available in stronger doses, by prescription only, as Motrin® and Rufen®. Other NSAIDs, available only with a prescription, are: ketoprofen (Orudis®), indomethacin (Indocin®), naproxen (Naprosyn®), mefenamic acid (Ponstel®), sulindac (Clinoril®), and piroxicam (Feldene®).

• Ozone, sulfur dioxide, nitrogen dioxide, cigarette smoke, carbon monoxide, hydrocarbons, nitrogen oxide and photochemical substances are air pollutants that can trigger asthma attacks. Follow the air pollution index reports in your area and stay indoors when the levels are high.

Back Problems

• Avoid moving suddenly. Sharp or sudden movements can aggravate back pain. Getting out of the car too quickly after sitting still for a long time or jumping up to answer the phone can be very dangerous for back problems. Learn to move slowly and carefully.

• Straining your neck muscles can aggravate your back. Don't hold the phone between your neck and your ear, even with a phone rest. Always hold the phone with your hand to avoid tensing up the neck muscles.

• Be careful when doing housework. We often underestimate how difficult housework is. Be sure to take breaks between doing heavy tasks. Stretch your back and neck muscles, as you would before exercising. By stretching them before the heavy tasks you will help prepare them and could avoid unnecessary muscle strain.

• Push, don't pull. Pulling heavy objects creates more strain on your lower back than pushing the object. If you suffer from back problems, don't be afraid to have plenty of help to move large objects.

• Move around frequently. Don't stay in one position for a long period of time. If you are driving, flying in an airplane or working at a desk, be sure to get up at least once each hour. Take a walk or change positions often.

• Always read in a comfortable position. Rest your arms on your lap, the arms of your chair, a table or a desk while reading.

• Take breaks from any repetitious activity. A woman suffered severe neck and back pain from doing needlework. Each night while cross-stitching, she held her head slightly to the side and did not support her arms. She remained in the same position for at least five hours each day. Now, after spending several weeks in a neck brace to reduce the pain, she cross-stitches only for short periods of time.

• Watch your posture. Don't slouch or sit in extremely soft chairs or couches. Be sure your back is properly supported whenever you are sitting or lying down. When driving or riding in a car, tilt the seat slightly forward. At first this position may feel awkward but it will give you better support and posture while in the car.

• Exercise. Regular exercise will help strengthen the back muscles so they will not be strained or aggravated by regular activities. When exercising, try to avoid sudden, jarring movements. Always warm up before starting vigorous exercise and use slow stretching exercises to cool-down afterwards. If using aerobic dance for exercise, try low-impact aerobics which keep at least one foot on the floor at all times, causing less jumping and jarring of the joints. A proper low-impact program will still give a good aerobic work-out while lowering the possibility of damaging your back.

• Strengthen your lower back muscles by holding in your stomach and buttock muscles to a count of ten. Release and tighten again. Repeat this several times each day to help strengthen the back muscles.

• To relieve lower back pain, soak in a warm bathtub or apply a heating pad directly to the back. Lie down on a firm surface and relax while applying gentle heat to the area. Avoid lying directly on a heating pad. It is best to put the heating pad on top of the body. If you must lie with it underneath, keep the heating pad on the lowest setting and use it for no more than 20 minutes.

• Many people with back problems pay frequent visits to chiropractors. Chiropractic treatment can hardly be called a natural way of dealing with physical problems, because it involves taking X-rays and manipulating the spine by a skilled practitioner. Some medical doctors claim that there is no value to chiropractic treatment and that most chiropractors are quacks. Some chiropractors respond that medical doctors don't care about the total well-being of their patients and often deal with them in a detached, impersonal manner.

I once asked a wise medical doctor what he thought of chiropractic treatment, and he told me that at least one-half of what physicians and other healers do is give the patient assurance that he's going to get better because of a particular type of treatment. Later, the patient often will get better, regardless of whether the treatment itself helped him.

This "placebo" effect is responsible for much of the healing that takes place regardless of what sort of treatment is used or what sort of practitioner used the treatment. According to my friend, the medical doctor, most chiropractors excel in the area of giving the patient confidence that he will get better because of their treatment.

When the "placebo" effect is combined with the body's own God-given ability to heal itself, the work of chiropractors, if they are sincerely interested in the welfare of their patients and if they are careful not to injure the spine, may sometimes surpass that of standard medical treatment.

There are not many good scientific studies on the effectiveness of chiropractic treatment. On the positive side, it seems to make some people feel better, and many people testify to this. On the negative side, medical doctors point out that it is quite possible to seriously injure the spine by manipulation and to cause injury to other parts of the body. One recent study by an M.D. showed that many elderly people experienced strokes soon after receiving chiropractic manipulation in the neck area. Medical doctors caution that spinal manipulation is less dangerous when it is performed in the lower back than when it is performed in the neck or upper back.

Baldness

Baldness usually occurs through a hereditary gene which is expressed most noticeably in males, although females may exhibit a small degree of hair loss late in life. There are certain remedies for baldness but they usually involve the application of drugs which often have side effects.

Estrogen creams rubbed on the head have been shown to reduce hair loss but they have caused feminizing side effects, such as enlargement of the breasts in many men who have used estrogen.

A new formulation of an old prescription drug, minoxidil (Loniten®), has been shown to greatly reduce hair loss. When taken internally, minoxidil (Loniten®) has been used to treat high blood pressure. But many people reported unwanted hair growth as a side effect of the drug. Researchers have developed a topical form of minoxidil (Rogaine®) that is rubbed directly into the scalp. In initial testing, Rogaine® was able to bring some new hair growth in many patients within two to twelve months of twice daily treatment, especially in causes of partial baldness. With the development of Rogaine®, other drug companies have increased their research into new hair regrowth products.

Natural means of avoiding hereditary baldness are less successful. The vitamins inositol and biotin taken internally or rubbed on the scalp in the form of ointments or shampoos may slightly reduce hair loss, but their effectiveness is quite limited.

Blindness (Night Blindness)

Loss of vision in near darkness is an early symptom of vitamin A deficiency. Vitamin A deficiency can be prevented by regularly eating yellow vegetables like carrots. Liver, eggs, and green leafy vegetables such as brocolli and spinach are also good sources of vitamin A.

Blood Clots

Many older people have a tendency to form blood clots in the legs and other parts of the body. Blood clots can be life-threatening if they block circulation or if they become dislodged and travel to the lungs or brain where they may cause a stroke.

Blood clots are less likely to form when people are active. Bedridden patients, like those recovering from surgery, should be encouraged to get up and walk. Patients who cannot walk should be encouraged to move around in bed or be turned frequently.

Avoid crossing your legs for long periods of time to help prevent clots from forming in the legs.

Vitamin E is reported to have an anti-clotting effect. It has been used to treat people with poor leg circulation, called intermittent claudication. People with intermittent claudication have a tendency to have leg cramps, experience pain when walking, and form blood clots in the legs.

Niacin (vitamin B3) is a blood-vessel enlarger. Niacin may improve circulation in the elderly, keep legs and arms from falling asleep, and help to prevent blood clots from forming. The overall effectiveness of using niacin to stop blood-clot formation is unknown and it may vary from person to person.

Niacin or vitamin E should only be used under the advice of a physician. Caution should be used in taking large doses which can cause serious side effects.

People taking prescription drugs to prevent blood clots should use caution when considering supplements of pantothenic acid (vitamin B5). Pantothenic acid supplements may reduce the effectiveness of blood thinning drugs.

Blood Pressure — High

High blood pressure is one of modern society's worst enemies. It usually increases with age. An estimated 60 million Americans have some form of hypertension (the medical term for high blood pressure). Although it is rarely listed on death certificates as the cause of death, high blood pressure, if left untreated, can lead to numerous other causes of death. Strokes, heart attacks, and kidney failures are major examples of the devastation of this elusive illness.

In most, but not all cases, high blood pressure can be lowered without prescription drugs. For example, in one recent university test, 85.3% of patients with high blood pressure were able to quit taking medication. Even without drugs, their blood pressures remained lower than when they were on drugs. The hundreds of people in the study also found that their blood cholesterol levels dropped 26%. The doctor in charge of the program said, "You lose your tiredness. You feel much more active. You have a general feeling of well being." The patients learned some of the health secrets described below and began making changes in their eating and exercise habits.

Common Causes of High Blood Pressure

Salt — Studies of different nations around the world show that high blood pressure is a problem only in societies where people eat a lot of sodium, usually in the form of salt. High blood pressure rates are in direct proportion to the amount of salt consumed. The more salt that a particular society consumes, the greater the number of cases of severe high blood pressure.

The average American eats five to ten grams of sodium per day, but most people only need one-tenth that amount. However, there are exceptions. Hard labor, pregnancy and breast feeding may increase the need for sodium to as much as 2 grams per day.

Most people will question whether they really consume one-third to one-fifth of an ounce of salt per day, but processed foods that Americans eat are usually filled with salt. Any food that comes in a can, a frozen package or a box is likely to have salt added as a preservative or flavor enhancer.

Many scientific studies show that reducing salt intake will lower blood pressure in most people by a significant amount. Getting salt intake down into the range of 500 mg. of salt per day helps the most. Reducing salt intake lowers blood pressure dramatically in some people who have a tendency toward severe high blood pressure because they have a hereditary tendency to hold on to salt or sodium. Thus, the benefits of reduced salt consumption are great for some of the people who need the benefits the most.

People on low-sodium diets should avoid taking sodium ascorbate. Sodium ascorbate is a formulation of vitamin C that contains sodium. If you need a vitamin C supplement while cutting back on sodium, ascorbic acid or calcium ascorbate forms of vitamin C are preferred.

Most people find that once they eliminate salt and get over the initial craving for salt, they don't miss it. A little creativity in your cooking can help add "spice" to your food while lowering the salt content. You do not have to sacrifice flavor when you cut down on sodium if you follow these suggestions from Prevention magazine:

> Use lemon juice on food instead instead of salt.

> When baking cakes, cookies, pies and puddings, use extracts instead of salt and reduce the sugar.

> Learn about the many natural herbs and spices that are available. You may decide to grow your own or to experiment with store-bought herbs.

> Use one of several salt-free mixtures of herbs and spices that are available for seasonings.

> Enjoy Mexican, Cajun, spicy oriental and Tex-Mex foods. The strong spices give flavor without adding salt.

> To spice chicken dishes, add fruit such as mandarin oranges or pineapples.

> Marinate chicken, fish, beef or poultry in orange juice or lemon juice. Add a mustard or honey glaze.

> Marinate meat in wine or add wine to sauces or soups. If you thoroughly cook the dish, the alcohol will evaporate but the flavor will be enhanced.

> Add unsalted nuts, sunflower seeds, sesame seeds or water chestnuts to any meat dish or salad.

> Just a little green pepper, parsley, paprika or red pepper can add a lot of flavor to a meal.

Tobacco — Avoid all forms of tobacco. Smoking is a well-known hazard to people with high blood pressure. Smoking cigarettes, pipes or cigars can constrict the arteries, which raises high blood pressure and increases the risk of heart failure. Chewing tobacco and snuff, also known as smokeless tobacco, should also be avoided because of their high salt content. According to an article in the New England Journal of Medicine (312: 919) the sodium levels in chewing tobacco and snuff are similar to the high levels found in dill pickles, which should also be avoided. Studies at Ohio State University have shown higher blood pressure levels in people who used smokeless tobacco, compared to nonusers. Smokeless tobacco also contains high amounts of licorice.

Black Licorice — Black licorice or licorice extracts should be avoided if you suffer from high blood pressure, according to researchers at Tufts University. Black licorice can make the body hold onto sodium (salt), lose potassium and cause fluid retention. People taking diuretics for their high blood pressure should be especially careful to avoid licorice because it seems to compound the problems and bad side effects of the diuretic drugs. About 90% of the licorice imported into the United States is used in chewing tobacco; this is another reason people with high blood pressure should avoid all forms of tobacco.

Vitamins Which Affect Blood Pressure — An overdose of vitamin D, from either excessive exposure to the sun, which acts on the skin to help produce vitamin D, or from taking high doses of vitamin D supplements, can lead to high blood pressure. Vitamin E, in doses larger than the RDA, can also cause high blood pressure.

Choline supplements are reported to help control blood pressure. In one study, one-third of a group of patients with high blood pressure had their blood pressure return to normal after receiving choline supplements. When the supplements were discontinued, their blood pressure rose once again. However, additional studies are needed to confirm that choline alone was responsible.

Cadmium and Lead— Cadmium is a "heavy metal" which may be found in small trace amounts in water supplies in the United States and in other countries. The cause and effect relationship between high levels of cadmium and high blood pressure exists as it does with salt. Studies indicate that other heavy metals, like lead, may also contribute to high blood pressure. Your local water authority may be able to tell you if your water supply has higher than average concentrations of cadmium or lead. If it does, certified pure bottled water would be a good alternative.

Drugs — Caffeine, diet pills and many prescription and over-the-counter drugs can raise blood pressure significantly. Caffeine is found in most "cola" and "pepper" drinks, coffee, tea and chocolate. Your pharmacist or your doctor can tell you if any prescription drugs you are taking can raise blood pressure. Also, be sure to read the warnings listed on any non-prescription medicines you may buy.

Pollution — Smog, smoking tobacco or breathing tobacco smoke has a significant effect in raising blood pressure.

We are all familiar with such pollution as smog, but do you know that excessive noise pollution raises blood pressure? It's true. Studies have shown that people who work in noisy environments have lower blood pressures after there is a significant reduction of noise in their environments.

Lack of Exercise — Many studies indicate that various types of exercise help to control high blood pressure. Exercise which increases the strength of the heart may help to prevent or lower high blood pressure. Aerobic exercise, such as jogging, swimming, walking and playing tennis can lower blood pressure. Also, surprisingly, isometric exercises which involve little body movement, are useful to reduce blood pressure.

Before starting an exercise program consult a physician and follow a recommended plan. Remember to slowly increase the intensity and duration of exercise. Don't overdo it in the beginning. Watch for body signals, such as sharp pains and cramps, that tell you when you're doing too much. Walking is usually recommended by doctors as the best beginning exercise for people who are out of shape.

Diets High In Fat — Americans now consume almost 40% of their total calories from fat. Cutting fat intake levels in half can have a dramatic effect in reducing many cases of high blood pressure. A recent study by the U.S. Department of Agriculture found that eating less saturated fat could bring blood pressure down even in the absence of taking other beneficial measures. Replacing saturated fats, which are found in meat and shortening, with vegetable oil or fish oil may also help reduce high blood pressure. Remember, fats are present not only in butter, oil and margarine, but also in fried foods, chips, creamed sauces, mayonnaise, pastries, and cheese to name a few. Learn to read labels on cans and packages, looking for the fat content listed.

Also see: **Cholesterol Reduction.**

Alcohol — Excessive alcohol drinking is the leading cause of high blood pressure among people who drink more than one ounce of alcohol (two drinks) per day. Alcohol makes blood pressure skyrocket as it damages the liver and kidneys and causes fluid build-up.

Family Environment — The disposition of your spouse or your partner's blood pressure has a great influence on your blood pressure levels. At the University of Texas, Marjorie A. Speers, Ph.D. discovered the relationship after examining over 1,200 couples (<u>American</u> <u>Journal</u> <u>of</u> <u>Epidemiology</u> May 1986). Other factors, like exercise, salt intake and obesity were taken into consideration, but the spouse still influenced the blood pressure levels. Perhaps a program for both the husband and the wife, including health care and counselling, could help in this situation.

False High Blood Pressure — Hardening of the arteries in the elderly may cause high, inaccurate blood pressure readings, Dr. Frank H. Messerli, a blood pressure specialist reported in the <u>New</u> <u>England</u> <u>Journal</u> <u>of</u> <u>Medicine</u>.

Messerli discovered that people over 65 with hardened arteries had higher blood pressure when monitored with a blood pressure cuff than their true blood pressure taken using a needle inside the arteries. Hardened arteries are caused by deposits in the arteries. Also see: **Coronary Heart Disease.**

Another kind of false high blood pressure is often called the "white coat syndrome". Many people, up to 30%, are diagnosed as having high blood pressure because they are nervous when their blood pressure is taken at their doctor's office. Home blood pressure readings, or 24-hour monitoring, can help give doctors a better picture of a patient's true blood pressure.

Natural Protection Against High Blood Pressure

Potassium— There is evidence that potassium may help protect against high blood pressure. Part of the evidence, however, is clouded by the fact that societies which have high levels of salt consumption also have low levels of potassium consumption and vice versa.

It may be beneficial and not at all harmful to eat more foods like bananas and citrus fruits, especially grapefruit, which are relatively high in potassium. Potassium supplements can be considered but should not be used by people who have kidney disease or who are taking a prescription diuretic that is potassium-sparing, because excessive potassium can be harmful or even fatal.

Calcium — Calcium supplements may help to lower some cases of high blood pressure. According to new research published in Drug Therapy (16,11:63), many people do not get enough calcium. Inadequate calcium can lead to high blood pressure. Another study indicates that people with high blood pressure consume 20 to 25% less calcium than people who don't have high blood pressure. Since taking calcium supplements or increasing the amount of calcium in the diet has few harmful side effects, extra calcium could be part of a blood pressure reducing therapy. However, do not stop taking blood pressure medication unless so advised by your doctor.

Dairy products, salmon, sardines and leafy green vegetables are the best natural sources of calcium. The RDA of calcium is 800 - 1200 mg. per day for adult males and females. Calcium supplementation should be avoided by people who have calcium oxalate kidney stones or by those with high blood-levels of calcium which make them more inclined to develop kidney stones.

Magnesium — A recent study by Dr. Burton M. Altura links low magnesium levels to high blood pressure. He believes that if the level of magnesium is too low, the calcium level becomes too high and the blood vessels contract, causing high blood pressure. In a separate study by Cornell University, Dr. Lawrence Resnick discovered that people with high blood pressure tend to have low magnesium in their red blood cells. Futhermore, Resnick claims that the patients who have their blood pressure under control have higher magnesium levels.

Other studies show that people have lower blood pressure if their water supplies have high concentrations of magnesium. Magnesium often is found with calcium in drinking water and in mineral supplements like Dolomite.

Breathing Exercises — Daily breathing exercises may help reduce high blood pressure. Practice by lying flat on your back on a carpeted floor. Prop up your head, and put a cushion under your knees so you are completely comfortable and relaxed. Breathe in slowly (to the count of ten), hold for two seconds, then breathe out slowly (another count of ten). Many people feel that they are practicing good breathing just by breathing in slowly, but slow exhaling is just as important. By doing these deep breathing exercises for only three to five minutes each day, you will feel relaxed and may lower your blood pressure and pulse rate.

Avoid the Valsalva maneuver — Avoid holding your breath when straining. This is called the Valsalva maneuver, and it often occurs during a bowel movement, while exercising or when you are trying to lift, pull, push or move something. Many times people hold their breath and grunt and groan when straining. However, holding your breath during these strenuous times causes your blood pressure to skyrocket and puts additional pressure on your heart and arteries. Practice breathing in and out slowly and steadily. Consciously breathe during any strenuous activity. Avoid all straining during bowel movements. The strain may cause hemorrhoids and bowel problems as well as increasing your blood pressure.

Love and Support — Although the doctor may never say, "Take one puppy and call me in the morning", many health professionals are now recommending the loving companionship and responsibility that a pet provides. According to medical studies, in some cases, having a pet can help people reduce their high blood pressure levels. Of course, pets aren't for everyone. They require care which some people cannot give.

One study shows that listening, rather than talking, lowers blood pressure. Most people experience a rise in blood pressure when they speak, followed by a rapid drop when they listen, reports <u>Arteries</u> <u>Cleaned</u> <u>Out</u> <u>Naturally</u>. The study indicates that the louder and faster a person talks, the higher the blood pressure. Learning to listen may lower stress and reduce the load on the heart.

Here are some tips for people taking medicine to control their high blood pressure:

> Get your blood pressure checked regularly; it takes only a minute or two. If it is above normal range (140/90), see your doctor.

> Take your prescribed medicine as directed. Keep doing so because even if you feel better, high blood pressure is not cured. Regular doses are necessary to keep it under control.

> Don't change the dose yourself. You might get too much or not enough medicine. Either way it could be harmful. If you

take less of your prescription than your doctor prescribes, you may increase the risk of complications such as stroke or heart attack. If you take more of your prescription than you're supposed to, you increase the risk of having side effects from the drug.

> Don't stop taking a drug "on your own", even if you feel lightheaded, dizzy, tired, depressed or have trouble sleeping. Your drug can be controlling your blood pressure but may also be giving you these or other side effects. Notify your doctor immediately when bothersome side effects occur. Many times your doctor will be able to switch you to another drug with less bothersome side effects. He needs to know how medication is affecting you, in order to treat your condition properly.

> If you have questions about your high blood pressure or your prescription, don't ask a friend or relative. Their information or advice may be well-intended but wrong for you. Ask your doctor or pharmacist — they are the people qualified to answer.

> Be sure to tell your doctor if you take other medicine regularly. Prescription drugs, vitamins, aspirin and other non-prescription drugs can interact with one another, causing decreased effectiveness or even dangerous side effects.

> Proper diet and exercise often help control high blood pressure. Consult your doctor to see how you can help lower your high blood pressure ... maybe to the point where drugs aren't needed!

> Some aging symptoms may be side effects of the blood pressure medication you are taking. Numbness in the hands, arms or feet, faintness upon rising, tiredness, dizziness, slow pulse, diarrhea, cold hands or feet, and dryness of mouth are common side effects of Inderal® and other beta blocking drugs used to help control high blood pressure. If you have any of these problems, discuss them with your doctor. He may be able to provide an alternative prescription that can help your blood pressure without these side effects.

> Inderal® and other beta-blocking drugs, prescribed to help lower high blood pressure, may cause depression, according to a study in the Journal of the American Medical Association (JAMA 255: 357-360). More than 20 percent of people taking beta-blockers eventually start taking antidepressant drugs, says Dr. Jerry Avorn of Harvard Medical School, who conducted the

study. Dr. Avorn says this is the first study that linked depression and beta-blockers, although many doctors have suspected a connection for several years. If you suspect your blood-pressure medication is causing depression, discuss alternatives with your doctor. Never stop taking a prescribed drug without your doctor's consent.

Blood Pressure — Low

People with low blood pressure often have difficulty standing up quickly. Because their bodies cannot quickly supply enough blood to the brain, they suffer from dizziness, fainting, light-headedness, blurred vision and shaking. Just as high blood pressure causes problems to the whole body, low blood pressure can be very dangerous.

Researchers at Vanderbilt University Medical Center in Nashville claim that coffee can help raise blood pressure that is too low. Many older people have trouble with low blood pressure, dizziness, fainting, or even collapsing after eating a large breakfast. Two cups of coffee, in the morning, seem to help combat all these symptoms. However, according to New England Journal of Medicine, for the coffee to be effective in the morning, it must be completely avoided for the rest of the day.

Breast Disease — Fibrocystic

About 20 percent of women between 25 and 50 years of age are thought to have fibrocystic breast disease. This disease produces non-cancerous breast lumps that cause soreness, swelling and pain in women, with the symptoms usually appearing just prior to monthly menstruation.

Many doctors are recommending elimination of caffeine and similar chemicals called methylxanthines to help relieve fibrocystic breast disease. Caffeine is found in coffee, tea, cola and pepper drinks, chocolate, and some prescription and over-the-counter drugs. However, in a recent article in the Archives of Internal Medicine, Drs. Wendy Levinson and Patrick Dunn at Good Samaritan Hospital in Portland, Oregon claim that there isn't any "good evidence" linking caffeine and fibrocystic breast disease.

Levinson and Dunn reviewed all the previous medical studies linking caffeine and fibrocystic breast disease and do not feel that women should routinely give up caffeine because of the fibrocystic disease.

Vitamin E has been used to reduce the non-cancerous swellings found in fibrocystic breast disease. Dr. Robert London of Baltimore discovered that 600 I.U.'s of vitamin E each day is helpful in reducing the disease in about 70 percent of affected women.

Breath — Shortness of

Shortness of breath due to stress or anxiety can be a very frightening experience. As we start to hyperventilate or "overbreathe," the level of carbon dioxide in the blood drops, and dizziness, lightheadedness, nausea and tingling sensations can begin. Trying to take slow, deep breaths may help at a time like this. Try inhaling as you silently count to 10, hold it for 5 seconds, then breathe out to another count of 10. At first, the breaths may be much shorter. However, if you concentrate and try to relax, deep breathing can restore the carbon dioxide level and relieve the problems.

Bruce Hensel, M.D. a professor at UCLA, suggests breathing into a paper bag for several minutes. The paper bag treatment will raise the carbon dioxide level. This is especially good for people who cannot achieve slow, deep breathing on their own.

If you wake up during the night because of shortness of breath, see your doctor as soon as possible. Sudden shortness of breath could be caused by asthma, a lung problem or heart trouble.

Bruises

Easy bruising may be caused by a deficiency of vitamin C, vitamin K or by poor absorption of vitamin K through the intestines which sometimes occurs with intestinal disease, especially as people grow older. Vitamin K is made by bacteria in the intestines and is found naturally in green, leafy vegetables, fruits, cereals, dairy products and meats. Vitamin C is obtained from citrus fruits, rose hips, acerola cherries, green peppers, parsley, broccoli, brussels sprouts, cabbage and potatoes.

Being bruised easily may also be a sign of a more serious health problem. You should see your doctor for his or her opinion.

Bunions

Bunions are a swelling or deformity of the big toe usually caused by improperly-fitting shoes. Most people who suffer from bunions are middle-aged. Bunions are especially common among older women who have worn tight, pointed-toe high-heeled shoes throughout most of their lives. In countries where high heels are not worn, like in Japan where until recently sandals were worn, bunions are infrequent. However, a few people may be genetically inclined to get bunions.

Here are some suggestions to help relieve the pain once a bunion appears:

> Wear only shoes or sandals that do not constrict your big toe and the wide part of your foot (called the toe box).

> Wear shoes with heels less than two inches high. If necessary, have your shoes widened or stretched by a shoe-repairer.

> Use small pads, like corn pads, which can be made especially for people suffering from bunions. The pads have a hole for the bunion and help to distribute pressure away from the area of the bunion.

Some exercises to stretch and strengthen the big toe and foot muscles may help alleviate some of the pain and help prevent the bunion from getting worse.

Bunions can be removed by surgery, but any surgery should be carefully considered and discussed with your physician.

Once a bunion is healed, do NOT go back to wearing tight-fitting, high-heeled shoes. Wearing comfortable shoes or sandals is the only way to help prevent bunions from recurring.

Burn Treatment

Serious burns should be treated by a physician. Minor burns may be treated at home only if the epidermis, the outer layer of the skin, is burned without blistering. Minor burns are classified as first degree burns. Second and third degree burns are the most serious.

Minor burns are usually caused by touching a hot object, exposure to hot water or steam, or a sunburn. According to The American Medical Association's Handbook of First Aid and Emergency Care, minor burns should immediately be placed under cold running water or covered by a cold compress to relieve the pain. Next the burn should be covered with clean bandages to protect it from infection.

The American Medical Association (AMA) does not recommend putting butter, grease, lard, ointments or any other substance on a burn without your doctor's recommendation.

For burns caused by a chemical, it is important to hold the burned area under cool running water for a minimum of five minutes. This is also true if an eye has been burned by a chemical. Flushing the area or the eye with water will help dilute the chemical and stop the burn from getting any worse. Flush the burn before calling a doctor or have someone else call for help, so the area can be cleansed as soon as possible.

Additional vitamin C may help healing after a burn, James Wasco, M.D., reports in Woman's Day magazine. Dr. Wasco recommends 500 mg. of vitamin C, twice daily, to help heal burns, fractures and damage to the body tissues.

Calluses — see: Corns and Calluses

Cancer

Cancer is an unrestrained growth of certain cells in the body. Some cancers are distributed throughout the body. Other cancers show up as tumors or clearly defined, rapidly growing masses of cells. Tumors can spread from one distinct location in the body to other locations.

Although cancer can affect people of all ages, we are more likely to develop it in our later years than when we are young. It is of special concern to the elderly because of the stresses cancer places on the body. Most deaths from cancer occur indirectly as a result of the cancer cells consuming the body's nutrients at a rate that is too fast for the body to keep up with. The healthy cells actually starve.

What Causes Cancer

There is no single cause of cancer, but there are many factors which can lead to its development. The first factor is a hereditary predisposition towards cancer. Because of their natural body constitution, some people are immune or more resistant to cancer than other people. A person whose constitution is not equipped to deal well with pre-cancerous changes will have a greater risk of getting cancer than other people.

The second major cause of cancer is radiation. Radiation from the sun is a proven contributor to skin cancer, particularly in fair-skinned people. People who spend a lot of time at the beach or working out in the sun have much greater rates of skin cancer than others. The early discoverers of radioactive materials often suffered from cancer because of working closely with these materials. People who have had excessive exposure to X-rays, particularly from X-ray machines which were manufactured several years ago, are at a greater risk of developing cancer.

The third major factor leading to cancer is exposure to cancer-causing environmental substances (carcinogens). The first substance noticed by medical science was soot from chimneys. Over a century ago, small children in England who were used as chimney sweeps often developed cancer of the testicles because of constant exposure to soot while climbing up and down chimneys.

Several decades ago, many scientists noticed that coal tar and coal tar products would cause cancer when applied to the skin of animals. Later, smoking and tar products from tobacco were proven to cause cancer.

Several decades ago, certain viruses were shown to cause cancer in animals. In recent years, viruses have been implicated in causing or contributing to the development of certain cancers in humans. The viral disease, hepatitis B, is the major cause of liver cancer. Herpes simplex virus has been implicated as a causative factor of cancer of the cervix in women. The Epstein-Barr virus can, under certain other environmental circumstances, lead to the development of Burkitt's Lymphoma. Viruses cause some leukemias. Only a small percentage of people who have been infected by certain viruses will actually get cancer.

Warnings Signs of Cancer

The American Cancer Society has developed a list of seven warning signs of cancer. Using the letters of the word CAUTION, they are easy to remember. If you notice any of these signs in yourself or a loved one, contact your doctor immediately. Early detection of cancer saves lives.

C —Change in the color or size of a wart or mole.

A—A sore that will not heal or is slow to heal.

U —Unusual, irregular or unexplained bleeding in the bowels, urine, nipples or vagina.

T —Thickening or lump in the breast, lip, tongue or elsewhere.

I—Indigestion or difficulty swallowing.

O—Obvious change in bowel or bladder habits.

N—Nagging or persistent cough or hoarseness.

Modern Treatment Methods For Cancer

Surgery, when appropriate, is the most effective treatment for cancer. If a tumor can be completely removed by surgery before it spreads, there may be a low rate of recurrence. Successful surgery depends upon detecting cancer at an early stage when a tumor may be small and easy to remove. Later on in the illness, the tumor may be very large and difficult to remove, or it may have spread into other areas.

Radiation and chemotherapy are sometimes successful treatments, particularly against cancers of the blood cells. Much of modern medical science is devoted towards improving forms of chemotherapy and radiation treatment. In spite of this effort, a recent study indicated that there is very little difference in survival rates for most types of cancers today than there was thirty years ago. Tumors have certain characteristics which make the body's immunity system ineffective in attacking them. Tumors seem to secrete protective "cocoons" which interfere with the natural defenses of the body's immunity system. Tumors may also give off antigens through these cocoons, and the body is fooled into attacking these "distractions."

The most promising area of research in cancer treatment is strengthening the body's immunity system so that the body itself can naturally attack the cancer which is growing inside it. Some researchers have reported success with various vaccines for certain cancers, like melanoma. Vaccines to prevent virus-caused disease may be effective in preventing cancer. A new vaccine for hepatitis B could reduce the chance of getting liver cancer by 90%. Vaccines have been given to people after surgery for lung cancer, and the results are still being evaluated.

One promising new treatment involves the injection of monoclonal antibodies which are specifically activated to attack the patient's own cancer cells. Other hopeful areas of research involve the injection of substances such as interleukin-3, interferon and enzymes like streptokinase to help the body's own defenses.

For the latest development in medical treatment of cancer, call this toll-free number 1-(800) 4-CANCER. This United States government sponsored information service can give you all the latest, up-to-date information.

Health Tips To Help Prevent Cancer

There are no natural cures for cancer once it becomes established, but there are many things that we can do to help prevent cancer and to reduce our chances of getting it.

•   Avoid cigarettes and other forms of tobacco. Tobacco tar is a potent, cancer-causing substance. When it's applied to the skins of experimental animals, it causes irritation which leads to higher rates of skin cancer in susceptible animals.

Cigarette smoke is the biggest environmental cause of cancer. People who smoke cigarettes or who live or work with people who smoke have higher rates of lung cancer and other cancers than other people. There are over 100,000 deaths from lung cancer in the United States each year. Most of these would never occur in the absence of breathing cigarette smoke.

In 1985, 60 non-smoking Canadian spouses died from lung cancer that is believed to have been caused by their spouses' smoking (Canadian Medical Association Journal).

As well as increasing your chances of getting lung cancer, smoking affects other types of cancers. Smoking increases a person's exposure to benzene by ten times, according to Medical

Update (10:9). Benzene is known to be a cancer-causing agent (a carcinogen) that can cause leukemia. Even non-smokers who live in the same house as a smoker are at an increased risk. They will receive 50% more benzene exposure than the average person. To avoid excessive benzene exposure, do not live or work in a smoke-filled environment.

Another recent study at the University of California found that smokers were twice as likely to develop cancer of the colon as were non-smokers. (Cancer 58:3,784).

People who are diagnosed as having any type of cancer need to give up smoking. A new study shows that nicotine actually speeds up cancer's growth in the body. Dr. Gesina Longenecker of the University of Southern Alabama School of Medicine, who made the discovery, recommends that all cancer patients quit smoking as soon as possible to slow down their cancer's development. Dr. Longenecker encourages cancer patients to quit smoking "cold turkey" rather than using a prescription gum called Nicorette® because the chewing gum also contains the dangerous nicotine which speeds up the cancer. Sadly, even though this advice is good, it's almost like closing the barn door after the horse has escaped.

The rate of lung cancer for ex-smokers goes down dramatically in the years following the time when they stop smoking.

• Avoid coffee. One study has shown that drinking many cups of coffee may lead to cancer of the pancreas. Another study by researchers at the National Institute for Health and Medical Research in France found coffee increased the risk of cancer of the pancreas regardless of how much coffee was consumed.

Also avoid decaffeinated coffee, except for decaffeinated coffee in which a water extraction process is used to remove the caffeine. Many manufacturers of decaffeinated coffee use a methylene chloride process which can leave a residue of this cancer-causing chemical in the coffee.

• Drink milk. In a recent study, people who didn't drink milk were three times as likely as milk drinkers to get colorectal cancer. The study was conducted by Chicago Western Electric Company, and researchers at the University of California in San Diego interpreted the data. Drinking two or three glasses of skim milk each day may help prevent colorectal cancer, according to this study. Don't take vitamin D supplements while drinking lots of vitamin D fortified milk, because of possible overdose of vitamin D which can be toxic.

•   Avoid excessive exposure to the ultraviolet rays from the sun. Both common skin cancer and a deadly form of skin cancer called melanoma are related to overexposure to the sun. Doctors warn that the development of skin cancer is on the rise as sun bathing has become popular. In 1982, one out of every 250 people developed skin cancer. But by the year 2000, one out of every 90 will develop it, forecasts Dr. Darrel Rigel of the New York University Medical Center.

Doctors suggest that everyone, especially people who spend a lot of time outdoors in the sunshine or people who are fair-skinned, should regularly examine themselves for warning signs of skin cancer. Active sunbathers, farmers, lifeguards, outdoor construction workers and sailors need to be particularly careful. A monthly "lookover" should include the body parts that are most often exposed, like your hands, face, neck, scalp and ears. According to the University of California, Berkeley Wellness Letter (3:9) watch for:

>   Changes in the color or size of a mole or wart.

>   A sore that will not heal or is slow to heal.

>   Any translucent growths on your skin. Usually this type of growth is shiny and white, pink or red in people with light-colored hair. Those with dark hair should be wary of darker, translucent growths.

>   Red patches on your skin. Sometimes these will crust or itch but other times you may hardly even notice them.

>   A smooth bump that is indented in the middle.

>   Any scar-like growths or spots, especially those that are white or yellow with a waxy surface.

New research at Cornell University suggests that ultraviolet rays actually destroy beta-carotene. Beta-carotene is used by the body to create vitamin A, which has natural anti-cancer properties and helps prevent lung cancer, bladder cancer and skin cancer.

Please protect yourself against skin cancer by using a sunscreen with a SPF (sun protection factor) of at least 12, and avoiding unnecessary exposure to ultraviolet light.

• Common skin tags may be a warning signal of colon cancer. Skin tags are small skin flaps, usually occurring in groups in the neck, armpits and groin areas. Until now, skin tags were thought to be harmless but cosmetically annoying. Researchers at the Mount Sinai School of Medicine in New York have discovered that 86 percent of their patients with colon cancer polyps also had skin tags. In further testing, 69 percent of their patients with skin tags, also had colon polyps. The researchers at Mount Sinai suggest that, to be safe, anyone with skin tags should have their stools checked for blood. You may want to ask your pharmacist about over-the-counter stool tests that can be done in the privacy of your own home. Since a stool test is a simple and inexpensive procedure, it would be best to be safe and have the test either at home or at your doctor's office.

• Protect your eyes. Like your skin, your eyes also need to be protected from the sun's ultraviolet rays. According to the New England Journal of Medicine (13, 313) cancer of the eye, called intraocular malignant melanoma, is mostly likely to occur in people who have spent a lot of time outdoors, especially sun bathers or those who use sun lamps. You can lower your risk to your eyes when outdoors by wearing special protective sun glasses (that protect against certain ultraviolet wavelengths), hats, or visors while in the sun. Sitting under an umbrella at the beach may protect you from direct sunlight, but the dangerous UV rays bounce off the sand and back under the umbrella. Even under an umbrella, you should still protect your eyes and wear a sunscreen to protect your skin.

• Avoid asbestos. Asbestos is a proven, serious cancer-causing material. Cigarette smokers normally have up to 10 times the rate of lung cancer as non-smokers, but cigarette smokers who also are exposed to asbestos particles in the air have rates of lung cancer up to 100 times higher than the rest of the population. Asbestos is such a serious cancer-causing agent that manufacturers of asbestos products have been sued to the point of bankruptcy by many people who have become cancer victims after handling their products.

Check for asbestos in your home. It was used in insulation, floorboard, wallboard, and plaster in homes and buildings constructed before 1972. As long as the asbestos is not disintegrating or flaky, it can be carefully covered and left intact. However, if any asbestos-containing material starts to disintegrate, a professional should be called in to remove it. If you have questions about asbestos in your home, office or school, you can call your local Environmental Protection Agency (EPA) office or 1-800-835-6700.

• Avoid using talcum powder in the genital areas. A study published a few years ago showed that women who use talcum powder in the genital areas or put it on sanitary napkins have a higher risk of ovarian cancer than those who don't use talcum powder. Talcum powder sold in foreign countries often contains asbestos, a proven cancer-causing substance. However, studies in the United States show that most brands of talcum powder sold here are asbestos-free or have a very low level of asbestos in them. This brings up the possibility that talcum powder itself, even if not contaminated with asbestos, may in some way lead to the development of cancer of the ovary.

• Avoid drinking or cooking with chlorinated water. Instead, use certified pure spring water. According to a report published by the U.S. Environmental Protection Agency (EPA) by Michael Alavanja, Inge Goldstein and Mervyn Susser, "residents of homes receiving chlorinated water had a higher risk of dying of cancers than those persons serviced by nonchlorinated water." The EPA has also identified and set standards on eight carcinogens (known cancer-causing substances) that are commonly found in drinking water. However, the EPA acknowledges that not all city or county water systems meet these standards. A number of other studies also indicate that drinking chlorinated water may be an important factor contributing to the cause of several kinds of cancer.

If you cannot afford spring water, trying boiling all water before using it or let the water sit out in an uncovered container for at least 24 hours so that chlorine, but unfortunately not harmful chlorinated hydrocarbons, will be released into the air and the water will be a little safer to use.

• Avoid fried foods. Eating fried foods can increase the risk of cancer because they usually contain high percentages of fat, often of the saturated variety, and because frying itself can change the cooking fat into even more harmful cancer-causing substances. If a person feels it is necessary to fry food, it is better to use unprocessed cooking oil such as peanut oil instead of margarine, shortening, or lard.

• High amounts of fat in your diet, if you are a woman, could double your chances of getting ovarian cancer, according to research from the Boston Hospital for Women. Women who drank skim milk, ate fish, and used margarine and vegetable fat had a lower incidence of ovarian cancer. Drinking whole milk and eating animal fat and butter increases the amount of fat in a woman's diet. Reducing the amount of fat in the diet may help lower the risk of ovarian cancer, says the study which was published in Obstetrics and Gynecology (63:833). This study supports the findings of Dr. David A Snowden from the University of Minnesota. In Dr. Snowden's study, women who ate eggs or fried foods died from ovarian cancer at three times the rate of women who avoided these foods.

• Dr. Snowden has also discovered an increased risk of prostate cancer in men who eat animal products as compared to men who follow a vegetarian diet.

• Fruits and vegetables may help protect you against certain types of stomach cancer according to research at the Louisiana State University published in the Journal of the National Cancer Institute (76: 4, 621). Eating crunchy yellow and dark green vegetables like broccoli, spinach, cauliflower and carrots, has received a lot of attention in the media, but eating other vegetables and fruits can also lower rates of stomach cancer. The study at Louisiana State found people who ate an above-average amount of fruit and vegetables were only HALF as likely to have a precancerous stomach condition called chronic atrophic gastritis. Increasing your intake of all fruit and vegetables is recommended.

• Vitamin C may play a role in the treatment or prevention of cancer. Vitamin C is an antioxidant that may slow down certain reactions, such as increased harmful peroxidation and free-radical formation. It is thought that free-radicals play a major role in causing cancer, heart disease, hardening of the arteries and aging.

Vitamin C may offer protection from some cancer-causing substances. Nitrates and nitrites, commonly used in food preservation, combine with amino acids in the body to form nitrosamines. Nitrosamines are thought to be cancer-causing substances. Vitamin C, according to Vitamin Side Effects

Revealed, is thought to prevent this combination from taking place. The National Academy of Science Committee on Diet, Nutrition and Cancer states: "Vitamin C can inhibit the formation of some carcinogens (cancer-causing substances) . . . The consumption of vitamin C containing foods is associated with a lower risk of cancers of the stomach and esophagus." In separate research, women with low levels of vitamin C were shown to have an increased incidence of precancerous abnormalities of the cervix.

Doctors are not necessarily recommending increased supplementation of vitamin C, but they do recommend eating more foods that are rich in vitamin C like rose hips, acerola cherries, citrus fruits, green peppers, parsley, broccoli, brussels sprouts, cabbage, honeydew melons, collard greens, kale, turnip greens, mustard greens, cauliflower and potatoes. Cooking causes 50-55% of the vitamin C to be lost, so raw fruit and vegetables are best. Fresh, refrigerated, or frozen juices have higher amounts of vitamin C than canned juices.

Terminal cancer patients, with cancer so advanced that other treatments had been abandoned, were given vitamin C. In studies by Linus Pauling, the patients who received the vitamin supplementation lived a few more months before dying (a dubious benefit shared by many terminal cancer patients given chemotherapy) than those not given vitamin C. If you have cancer, do not stop or change the treatment prescribed by your doctor, but you may want to discuss the benefits of vitamin C supplementation.

• Eat foods rich in vitamin D, calcium, molybdenum and selenium, such as fish, whole grain foods, wheat germ and beans. Studies have shown high rates of cancer in people who have a low supply of these nutrients in their diet.

• Cancer tumors in the mouth can be reduced or prevented by beta-carotene, based on the results of preliminary research at Harvard University. Beta-carotene is a natural substance found in fruits and vegetables, especially in yellow vegetables like carrots. The healthy human body produces vitamin A from beta-carotene. According to the Harvard study, published in the journal Carcinogenesis, cancer tumors in hamsters' mouths disappeared within two weeks after a beta-carotene solution had been applied directly onto the tumors or injected into the tumors. Other research, including more work at Harvard, has shown that people who eat fruits and vegetables high in beta-carotene seem to have a lower than normal incidence of cancer.

• Foods rich in vitamin E or beta-carotene may help defend you against lung cancer, reports The New England Journal of Medicine. People with low blood levels of vitamin E were 2 1/2 times more likely to get lung cancer. Low levels of beta-carotene could increase your chances of getting lung cancer by four times, concludes a study from Johns Hopkins University. Another study by the State University of New York at Buffalo confirmed the link between beta-carotene and lung cancer. The difference between the diet of lung cancer patients and healthy individuals was the amount of beta-carotene as found in one carrot eaten each day, the study reported in the American Journal of Epidemiology (125:3,351). Whole grains and nuts contain high amounts of vitamin E. Yellow or orange vegetables or fruits, like carrots, are particularly good sources of beta-carotene, which the healthy body converts to vitamin A.

• Calcium supplements may reduce the risk of colon cancer according to research by Dr. Martin Lipkin at the Memorial Sloan-Kettering Cancer Center. In these tests, calcium helped lower precancerous changes in the bowel and may have helped reduce the occurrence of stomach cancers.

• Eat cereals and whole grain products. These foods contain dietary fiber which helps move waste products through the intestines rapidly so that they won't turn into cancer-causing substances and stay in contact with the lining of the intestine for long periods of time. Dietary fiber can reduce the chances of getting certain kinds of cancer. This has been shown to be true for not just cancer of the colon, but many other kinds of cancer as well.

Your fiber intake should be at least 30 grams each day and include a variety of fiber types, according to the National Cancer Institute. A new study from Texas A & M University shows that too much "mushy" fiber may lead to colon cancer. High quantities of three types of fiber, pectin (found in fruits and root vegetables), guar (found in processed foods and ice cream) and oat bran, were found to contribute to the development of colon cancer. These mushy types of fiber help to lower cholesterol, but they slow down movement through the intestines. Harder types of dietary fiber, like bran, help move waste products through the intestines rapidly. With less contact with the lining of the intestines, the cancer-causing substances in the intestines seemed to be less harmful. While fiber is generally beneficial, too much of a *single type* of fiber such as psyllium mucilloid supplements should be avoided. For the best overall effect, you diet should include a variety of miller's bran, oat bran, fruits, vegetables, whole-grain breads and cereals.

• Cereals and whole grain products contain the mineral selenium which may help to prevent cancer. Population studies have shown that areas of the country where selenium is high in food or in the water have low rates of cancer. Selenium is part of an enzyme in the body which may help combat or prevent cancer.

Men should consume plenty of selenium according to studies conducted in The Netherlands (American Journal of Epidemiology 125,1:12). In the study at Erasumus University in Rotterdam, men with cancers were found to have "significantly lower" levels of selenium in their blood than men without cancer. However, there was no difference in the blood levels of selenium in women. It is recommended that adults consume 50 to no more than 200 micrograms of selenium daily from foods. Excessive selenium can be poisonous. Natural selenium sources include liver and other organ meats, seafood, eggs, onions, meat, poultry, grains, cereals, dairy products and vegetables. Selenium is an antioxidant which may help to protect against cancer as it fights free radicals in the body.

• Substances found in garlic and onions are now being studied to see if they can slow cancer growth. Dr. Michael Wargovich at the University of Texas has shown that organic sulfides in garlic and onions slow the progress of colon cancers in experiments. Be careful about increasing the amount of garlic and onions that you eat, though. Eating them in large quantities can have some unpleasant side effects like bad breath.

• Include lysine in your diet. A recent study commissioned by the Benjamin Franklin Literary and Medical Society showed that people who took supplements of the amino acid, lysine, had much lower rates of cancer than other people. Interestingly enough, in the study there was no significant reduction in rates of cancer for people who took extra selenium, zinc, vitamin E, vitamin C and vitamin A. Taking these supplements has been suggested for cancer prevention. For people who prefer not to take supplements, skim milk is a good source of protein which contains lysine in relatively high amounts.

• Iron deficiency has been linked to stomach and esophageal cancers, according to Nutrition and Health (8:6). Because excess iron is NOT eliminated from the body, researchers recommend consuming iron-rich foods rather than taking iron supplements. Whole-grain products, liver, organ meats, red meat, eggs, lima beans, prunes, spinach, raw broccoli, peas, fish, soy products and raisins are all good natural sources of iron.

• Adequate amounts of the mineral molybdenum are also important in reducing the risk of stomach and esophageal cancers, reports Nutrition and Health (8:6). Molybdenum is naturally contained in whole-grain products, dark green leafy vegetables and legumes.

• Do not eat apples, sour cherries or peanuts that have been treated with daminozide (trade name is Alar® by Uniroyal). Daminozide, a chemical used to keep apples red, delay ripening and increase their shelf-life, is absorbed by the apple and becomes incorporated into the fruit. **Washing or peeling the apple will not remove it.** According to the Food and Drug Administration (FDA), daminozide can cause cancerous tumors of the uterus, liver, kidney, blood vessels and lungs. Some stores and large baby-food manufacturers are now refusing to carry daminozide-treated products. You can't tell by inspection which apples have been treated, so buy only from stores and companies who refuse to sell daminozide-treated apples. American Health (16:4) recommends eating all fresh apples raw, since cooking seems to increase daminozide's cancer-causing properties.

• Small quantities of jalapeno and cayenne peppers may help reduce the risk of cancer, according to a report from Dr. Peter M. Gannett of the Eppley Institute. These hot peppers contain capsaicin, which is changed into a chemical that absorbs free radicals in the liver. Free radicals are thought to cause cancer, so capsaicin may help reduce cancer. However, since large amounts of capsaicin can cause changes in blood pressure, brain damage and stomach ulcers, only small amounts of peppers are recommended.

- Avoid processed foods which may have additives that can contribute to the development of cancer. It's good to avoid all artificially colored foods because they may contain certain food dyes which are suspected of causing cancer. Read the labels of food products, especially processed meat products, to find out if they contain food dyes.

Most processed meats and most red meats have sodium nitrite added to act as a preservative and red-coloring agent. Bacon, hot dogs and processed meats contain large amounts of this preservative. Sodium nitrite can react with other chemicals in the body to form cancer-forming substances called nitrosamines.

Eliminate or consume only small amounts of food that is smoked, salt-cured, pickled, cooked over wood or charcoal, or treated with nitrites. According to the Nutrition and Health newsletter from Columbia University (8:6), these foods increase the risk of developing stomach or esophageal cancer. Certain sausages, ham and fish readily absorb the tars from smoke or charcoal. These tars contain substances which are known to cause cancers. People should also be especially careful when traveling in China or Japan because pickled and salt-cured foods are very common there.

Some foods are naturally high in nitrates including raw beets, cauliflower, broccoli and cabbage. Raw spinach, lettuce, pumpkin and kosher salami are high in nitrites.

To further reduce your risk of cancer, the American Institute for Cancer Research (AICR) recommends:

> Eat less than four ounces total of salt-cured, nitrite-cured, smoked, processed meats or charcoal-broiled foods per week.

> When eating salt-cured, nitrite-cured, smoked or charcoal-broiled foods, also eat foods rich in vitamin C. Vitamin C is an antioxidant that may help reduce the effect of the nitrosamines in the body.

> Wrap meat, fish or poultry in aluminum foil before grilling it on charcoal.

> Baste or marinate all foods that are going to be cooked over charcoal.

> Do not eat meat that is charred.

> Do not eat crispy bacon. Bacon cooked in a microwave contains the least amount of dangerous nitrosamines.

> Throw away animal fats and oils rather than using them in soups, gravies or cooking. Some pesticides become concentrated in animal fat and the fats may be more dangerous than the meat.

• Avoid artificial sweeteners. Artificial sweeteners containing saccharin have been shown to cause bladder cancer in animals. At present, a number of studies indicate that these same products are fairly safe in humans. Nevertheless, a few studies indicate that bladder cancer in humans, and particularly in human males, may be increased by consuming large amounts of artificial sweeteners containing saccharin.

There is at present no evidence that artificial sweeteners which contain aspartame (brand name Nutrasweet®) cause cancer in animals or in humans.

• Reduce or eliminate tea from your diet. According to a study in Hawaii, men who drank tea more than once a day had a four times greater risk of developing rectal cancer than men who "almost never" drank tea. (British Journal of Cancer 54:5,677). The test included tea made from black tea leaves which had been brewed to make tea. It did not differentiate between hot or iced tea. If you experience **any** anal irritation after drinking tea, stop drinking it immediately. Other medical studies have shown a connection between drinking tea and developing kidney, pancreas or bladder cancer.

• Avoid alcohol. People who consume high quantities of alcohol have higher rates of cancer than other people. Alcohol may play a direct role in contributing to the development of such cancers as liver cancer. Also, it may take the place of other foods which contain vitamins and other substances which help the body fight and prevent cancer. In other words, alcohol may contribute to cancer development by causing nutritional deficiencies because it displaces other foods.

A recent study published in The New England Journal of Medicine (316:1169) showed that women who drank even moderate amounts of alcohol had a greater risk of developing breast cancer than women who did not drink.

• Avoid barrier forms of contraception, like condoms. A scientific study (Oncology 35(3): 97-100) has shown that 71% of women who had breast cancer surgery had used barrier contraception, but only 34% of the control group had used this method. Estimates based on these studies indicate that 16% of all women who use barrier contraception and who do not have breast cancer will develop it at some point in the future. Only 3.4% of married women who don't use barrier contraception will develop breast cancer.

• Exercise has been proven to lower your risk of getting certain cancers, according to the New England Journal of Medicine (314:10,605). Women who participated in college sports and continue to exercise regularly have a lower incidence of uterine, vaginal, cervical, ovarian and breast cancer than women who are not exercising. This study by Harvard University's Grace Wyshak, Ph,D. and Rose Frisch, Ph.D., involved over 5,000 women.

Having a desk job may increase the risk of getting colon cancer by 30% according to two recent studies. State University in Buffalo, New York found that men with inactive jobs were twice as likely to get colon cancer compared to men who had active jobs. The Swedish National Institute of Environmental Medicine discovered that men who sat down for more than half of the work day had a 30% higher rate of colon cancer than men who were more physically active on the job (New England Journal of Medicine 313:22, 1381-4). It seems that long periods of sitting allows the body's waste, and the cancer causing substances in it, to collect in the colon for longer periods of time. Extra concern for a proper, high-fiber diet and plenty of exercise should be a top priority for both men and women with desk jobs.

• Cleaning supplies, bleach, paint, paint removers, oven cleaners, floor polish, and pesticides should be kept away from living areas if possible. Many of these products contain methylene chloride, a suspected carcinogen that has produced cancerous tumors in laboratory animals, reports the Consumer Federation of America.

• Check for radon gas. According to the Environmental Protection Agency (EPA), high levels of radon gas in homes may be the second leading cause of lung cancer. Radon gas is a radioactive byproduct of uranium that has been found in over 30 states. It is a gas that can seep into a house through concrete floors, floor drains, cracks, or through your water if you have a private well. To check your home's radon gas level, call the local EPA or health department. To reduce exposure to radon gas keep your house well-ventilated and limit the amount of time you spend in the basement where the gas levels are usually higher. Do not allow smoking in your home since radon can attach to the small particles of tobacco smoke where they can be inhaled directly into the body and trapped in the lungs.

• Consider where you live. Like radon gas, living close to large chemical plants, polluted water, waste disposal areas, certain industries or natural deposits of minerals could increase your risk of getting cancer. Learn more about your neighborhood. If the risk of getting cancer is increased, you may want to relocate.

• Limit or eliminate the use of pesticides inside the home. A recent study in the Journal of the National Cancer Institute showed that children in homes where indoor pesticides were used once a week were 3.8 times more likely to develop leukemia. If pesticides were also used regularly in the garden or elsewhere outside, the children's risk of developing cancer increased to 6.5 times compared to unexposed children.

• Avoid exposure to harmful substances. According to Time's Symptoms and Illnesses, lung cancer is often caused by exposure to:
> asbestos
> chromium
> nickel
> iron
> petroleum oil mists
> cigarette, cigar and pipe smoke
> isopropyl oil
> coal tar fumes
> air pollution
> radioactive substances

• Rectal cancer may be influenced by the level of cholesterol in the blood. According to Swedish research published in The New England Journal of Medicine (315:26,1629), high levels of cholesterol increased the risk of developing rectal cancer by 1.65 times over average levels. Another study in the same issue of the journal reports that people with high levels of cholesterol were twice as likely to develop colon polyps as people with low cholesterol levels.

All men over 50 years of age should have a yearly rectal exam for signs of prostate and other cancers since the incidence is highest in this age group.

• See the doctor if you experience prolonged stomach irritation like heartburn, nausea, bloating, loss of appetite, belching or mild pain because these could be the first signs of stomach or esophageal cancer.

• Take steps to lower your blood pressure. In people with cancer, the higher their blood pressure, the more likely they are to die from the cancer, reports the Journal of the National Cancer Institute (77:1,63).

• Cervical cancer can be treated effectively if it is diagnosed early. If women have an annual PAP smear, they reduce their risk of developing undetected cancer of the cervix.

• Women who have been on oral contraceptives (the "pill") for a minimum of 12 consecutive months seem to have a lower risk of developing endometrial cancer. According to a study by the Centers for Disease Control in Atlanta, the risk of getting endometrial cancer is cut in half in some women who have used the "pill" (Journal of the American Medical Association JAMA 257:6,796). However, the researchers warn that even with the benefits of lower incidence of cancer, women who smoke should not take oral contraceptives because of the increased risk of heart and artery problems.

Women who have an increased risk of developing endometrial cancer should be sure to have a gynecological exam at least once a year. The risk of developing endometrial cancer (in the lining of the uterus or womb) increases if the woman:

> does not ovulate
> is infertile
> is obese
> has diabetes
> had a late menopause
> had long-term estrogen therapy after menopause.

• The risk of breast cancer is slightly higher in women who have estrogen-replacement therapy (ERT), reports the Centers for Disease Control (CDC) in Atlanta (Journal of the American

Medical Association JAMA 257,2, 209). However, they suggest that women and their doctors need to weigh the proven benefits of estrogen-replacement therapy (protection against osteoporosis and heart or artery problems) against the slightly increased risk of breast cancer. Women who have a family history of breast cancer should probably avoid estrogen-replacement therapy, the study concluded.

High amounts of protein in a woman's diet could increase her chances of developing breast cancer according to research by Dr. E.J. Hawrylewicz of Chicago's Mercy Hospital. The American Institute for Cancer Research (AICR) reports that Dr. Hawrylewicz discovered that "feeding laboratory animals high protein diets generally increases their susceptibility to breast cancer when they are exposed to a carcinogen."

Women with a history of breast cancer in their families should be especially careful to give themselves monthly breast exams and have regular breast exams and mammograms by their physicians. According to statistics from the Centers for Disease Control in Atlanta (Journal of the American Medical Association JAMA 253 :1908), women who have a mother **and** a sister with breast cancer have 14 times the normal risk of developing breast cancer. If a grandmother or aunt has had breast cancer, their risk is 1.5 times greater than average. If a mother **or** a sister has had it, the risk is 2.3 times greater. Women with a family history of breast cancer should alert their doctors. Careful screening and early detection should help keep an occurrence of breast cancer as limited as possible.

In a monthly exam, a woman's breasts need to be checked for all warning signs of cancer, not just lumps. Dr. James Wasco, M.D., a columnist for Woman's Day magazine, reports that several other things can be possible warning signals. As you begin regular breast exams, you will be able to catch any changes much earlier than your doctor. You will be familiar with the shape, normal lumps and coloring of your own breasts. During your monthly self-exam watch for:

> Any change in the shape, size or color of the breasts. Do this by comparing them in a mirror each month. Compare them to each other and to how they looked in the previous month.

> Any unusual discharge should be noted and reported to

your doctor.

> Scaliness or crustiness on the breasts, especially around the nipple.

> Any new dimples in the breasts.

> Any lumps or thickening of the breast tissue.

> Asymmetry — any difference in the shapes of the breasts.

The American Cancer Society now recommends that women 50 and over, even if they don't have cancer or breast problems, should have a mammogram once every year. Women between 40 and 49 should have a mammogram every second year. The first mammogram should be given when a woman is between 35 and 39 years of age. The first mammogram is used as a base line to detect any irregularities later, the Society explains. A mammogram is a special low-dose X-ray of the breast which enables doctors to detect the "earliest and most curable breast cancer". Some women are at a high risk for developing breast cancer. If you fall into one of the high risk categories listed below, you should ask your doctor or gynecologist for regular mammograms:

> if you gave birth to your first child after the age of 30.

> if you have never given birth.

> if your mother or sister has developed breast cancer.

> if you reached sexual maturity very early.

> if you have a history of cysts in your breasts.

> if you are overweight.

> if you are over 40 years of age.

• Avoid laxatives containing danthron. Danthron has been proven to cause colon and liver cancer in animals. It was contained in these common laxatives until May 1987: Modane® (Regular, Mild, Liquid and Plus), Doxidan®, Dorbantyl®, Dorbane®, Guarsol®, Danthron tablets, Key Lax® Laxative Tablets, Docusate Calcium® with Danthron and DC® with Danthron. The Public Citizens Health Letter (3:4), a Ralph Nader newsletter, suggests that you throw away any laxatives you have which contain danthron or return them to your pharmacist for a refund. Products containing danthron have been banned in Britain and the United States but some people may still have these products in their medicine cabinets.

Canker Sores

A canker sore is a tiny, raw ulcer located on the tissue inside the mouth. They are usually quite painful and can occur inside the cheeks or lips, on the gums, and under the tongue.

Some doctors believe that canker sores are caused by a deficiency of vitamin B12 (cobalamin), iron and folic acid. Vitamin B12 is found naturally in liver, meat, milk, dairy products, fish and eggs. It is virtually absent in vegetables. Many vegetarians who do not eat meat or eggs may have a vitamin B12 deficiency. Folic acid is found in yeast, liver, lima beans, whole-grain products, leafy green vegetables, asparagus, beans, turnips, peanuts, oats, potatoes and oranges. Folic acid and vitamin B12 work together. If there is a low amount of one of these vitamins, the other one will not work as well. Iron is found in whole-grain products, liver, organ meats, red meat, eggs, lima beans, prunes, spinach, raw broccoli, peas, fish and raisins.

A diet high in lysine and low in arginine may help reduce canker sores. Studies at Indiana University School of Medicine and at UCLA have found that lysine helps repress the sores and arginine promotes their growth. Both lysine and arginine are amino acids. Dairy products and yeast are high in lysine. Nuts, seeds, chocolate and some cereals are high in arginine and low in lysine and should be avoided, according to the research. Some doctors recommend lysine supplements up to 1,200 milligrams daily to stop canker sores.

Cataracts

Cataracts develop when the lens of the eye becomes cloudy; this often happens with advancing age. A cataract may start when one of the body's enzyme systems, which helps keep the lens of the eye clear, performs less efficiently as the person gets older. Factors contributing to the development of cataracts are:

> Exposure to ultraviolet light. Wearing sunglasses in bright sunlight or avoiding bright sunlight may be helpful in preventing cataracts. The Western Journal of Medicine (144:454) reports that only sunglasses which properly filter out the ultraviolet rays are effective in protecting the eyes. Common sunglasses may prevent bothersome glare or brightness but not fully protect against ultraviolet light.

> Riboflavin (vitamin B2) deficiency may be one cause of cataracts. There are reports of cataracts diminishing after supplements of riboflavin were taken but these claims are unconfirmed. Caution: Don't take more riboflavin than the Recommended Daily Allowance (RDA). Overdoses of B vitamins may promote the development of cataracts.

> Taking large doses of niacin (vitamin B3) or other B vitamins may increase the chances of getting cataracts.

> A recent study has shown that people who regularly take acetaminophen or aspirin have half the rate of cataracts as people who don't take these over-the-counter pain relievers.

> Any vision changes should be reported to a physician. Most cataracts can be corrected or arrested with surgery.

Chills

If you get a chill, check with your doctor because they are often a symptom of a serious disease, infection or poor circulation.

> Chills can be caused by vitamin D overdose. This can occur after taking a large amount of a vitamin D supplement or after excessive exposure to sunlight. In addition, sunburn causes the skin to redden and lose heat, causing further chilling. Excessive sunlight makes the skin produce large amounts of vitamin D.

Also see: **Cold Sensitivity.**

Cholesterol Build-Up

• Lowering blood cholesterol levels can reduce the rate of coronary heart disease and hardening of the arteries. Researchers have observed that the levels of fats in the blood can be lowered by changes in the diet. As early as 1947, a study of heart disease in seven nations showed a direct relationship between a country's incidence of heart disease, the level of cholesterol in the blood and the amount of animal fat in the national diet.

• According to the Coronary Prevention Trial at the Lipid Research Clinic, each 1% drop in the serum cholesterol level can lower the risk of having a major heart attack by 2%. For example, a five-percent reduction in blood-cholesterol levels should reduce coronary heart disease rates by ten-percent.

• The first step in lowering blood cholesterol levels is diet therapy and weight loss if you are overweight. A moderate exercise program may also be helpful. The dietary approach is to lower total fat, saturated fat and cholesterol consumption. Here are some practical suggestions for a healthier diet.

> Do not consume more than 100 milligrams of cholesterol for each 1,000 calories. Daily cholesterol should not exceed 300 milligrams.

> Eat chick-peas, soy-bean products, oats, and carrots to help maintain low cholesterol levels. Oat bran is an excellent source of water-soluble fiber and can reduce blood cholesterol levels by 6 to 19%, based on data from the Lipid Research Clinic. Researchers at Northwestern University (Journal of the American Dietetic Association) discovered that about two cups of oatmeal or two oat bran muffins daily, combined with moderate levels of dietary fat and cholesterol, can lower cholesterol levels in just a few weeks. If you prefer oat bran muffins, be sure to use a low cholesterol substitute, rather than eggs, in the muffins.

For best overall health, also eat foods like fruit, bran, whole grain breads and cereals. These foods may not lower cholesterol as well as oat bran does, but they are better than oat bran for preventing colon cancer and other diseases.

> Saturated fats, found in red meats and dairy products, should be reduced to less than 10% of total calories. Foods that are rich in cholesterol should be avoided or drastically limited in the diet. These foods include egg yolks, organ meats and most cheeses. Foods that should be reduced because they are high in saturated fats include: butter, bacon, beef, whole milk, cream, chocolate, almost any food of animal origin, hydrogenated vegetable shortenings, coconut oil and palm oil.

> Unsaturated fats, such as fish and vegetable oils, may constitute as much as 10% of total calories.

> Total fat intake should be less than 30% of your daily calories.

> One of the best sources of polyunsaturated fats is fish, especially cold water fish like salmon, trout, tuna, mackerel and cod. Researchers are discovering that omega-3 fatty acids found in

fish oils actually lower levels of cholesterol and other blood fats associated with heart disease (New England Journal of Medicine 312:19,1210-16).

Unfortunately, the canning process destroys most of the important oils in these fish. It is better to increase the amount of fish in your diet without relying on canned fish. Eating fresh, cold-water fish like salmon, trout, tuna, herring, mackerel and cod twice a week will provide plenty of healthful fish oils without having to take "possibly dangerous" fish oil supplements (International Journal of Epidemiology 6/86).

> Until studies have proven their safety, doctors in the New England Journal of Medicine (316:10,626) report that it is probably better to eat fish than to take fish oil supplements. Supplements can cause diarrhea and increase bleeding time, according to The Medical Letter (29:731). Cod liver oil, especially, should be avoided because it contains cholesterol and can lead to overdoses of vitamins A and D, according to a report from Dr. Nathaniel Shafer of New York Medical College in the Medical Tribune.

Other researchers, including Harry S. Glauber of the University of California at San Diego, report that fish oil capsules can actually raise blood sugar levels in diabetics. People with inactive diabetes may discover that the fish oils activate the problem, Glauber says. He recommends that diabetics and people at high risk for developing diabetes should avoid the supplements.

> Salmon oil can reduce the blood's ability to clot. DO NOT take salmon oil supplements with aspirin treatment or prior to surgery.

> Daily garlic may be good for you by helping to reduce the levels of LDL (low-density lipoprotein) cholesterol in the blood, and by raising the level of beneficial HDL (high-density lipoprotein) cholesterol; according to a study in The American Journal of Clinical Nutrition, this lowers the chances of blood clots. The study used specially extracted garlic oil which was equivalent to eating 10 cloves of garlic daily. In six months, the level of HDL cholesterol (the "good" type of cholesterol that can help prevent coronary heart disease) was increased by 41%. However, eating ten regular cloves of garlic daily could provide some unwanted side effects like bad breath, diarrhea and body

odor. Unfortunately the garlic pills, oils and extracts currently sold in health food stores do not contain the necessary ingredients to help in the cholesterol battle.

> Try to avoid artificial and non-dairy creamers. If you need to use a powdered product (due to lack of refrigeration) use low-fat powdered milk. The instant, non-fat dry milk is convenient and has a lower fat content than a non-dairy cream substitute.

> Don't use foods containing coconut or palm oil. They are high in saturated fats.

> Cut back on beef, lamb and pork. Never eat any combination of them more than three times per week.

> Don't eat duck or goose. Both are high in fat content.

> If you must eat beef, use only lean cuts. When cooking at home, cut off all visible fat. Broiling, baking or roasting the meat in its own juices are the healthiest methods of preparation. When eating out, select the best quality cuts like a filet mignon or chateaubriand. Keep your portions small and don't use any gravy or sauce. Also, avoid casseroles and pot pies.

> When preparing chicken or turkey, be sure to cut off the skin because much of the fat is contained in the skin. Eat the light meat on a turkey or chicken because it contains less fat than the dark meat.

> When eating red meat, serve less meat by preparing dishes that use meat plus vegetables, pasta or grains. Then you can use less meat per person while still providing adequate protein, vitamins and minerals. Stir-frying strips of meat with vegetables or cooking them in a wok is a good example.

> For dishes that require hamburger, substitute ground turkey (without the skin) or, if you are a hunter, you may want to substitute ground venison.

> Don't buy meat, fish or poultry that is already breaded. If you want to bread the meat, make your own breading with plain bread crumbs, herbs, skim milk and egg whites. Don't deep-fry after breading.

> Avoid prepared luncheon meats. As well as being high in fat, they are high in sodium and nitrites. Sliced turkey breast, tuna salad and salmon salad (without mayonnaise) are good luncheon alternatives.

> When making soup, chili, or stew, place the broth in the

refrigerator overnight. In the morning, remove any fat that has hardened at the top.

> Eliminate bacon bits from your diet. In salads and soups, try homemade croutons or herbs to add that "spicy" taste.

> Limit your egg yolks to two per week. This includes not only whole eggs, but eggs used in baking and cooking. To reduce cholesterol, <u>Cardiac Alert</u> (9:5) recommends using two egg whites instead of one whole egg in cooking and baking.

> If you are using egg substitutes in trying to reduce your cholesterol intake, be careful. Many commercial egg substitutes are high in sodium or high in fat, even though they may be cholesterol-free.

The American Heart Association recommends making a cholesterol-free egg substitute especially for use in baking: Beat three egg whites. Then add 1/4 cup non-fat milk, 1 tablespoon non-fat dry milk powder, and 1 teaspoon of polyunsaturated vegetable oil. Mix these four ingredients together to make a healthful egg substitute. According to an avid cholesterol-watcher, if you add a drop of yellow food coloring when making French toast, your family won't be able to tell the difference!

> Pre-packaged cake mixes, biscuits and pancake mixes are usually made with eggs. To make your own easy mix, combine all the necessary dry ingredients together and freeze. When you want to bake them, just take your mix out of the freezer and add the liquids. For the liquids, use only egg substitutes, non-fat milk and vegetable oils.

> When buying pasta, avoid noodles made with eggs.

> Avoid crackers that contain lard or "animal fat". Study the list of ingredients and buy only crackers made with acceptable vegetable oils. If a cracker leaves a grease stain on a paper towel, it contains too much lard

> Avoid croissants.

> When buying bagels, choose those made with water rather than eggs.

> Switch from butter to margarine, preferably soft margarine.

> Don't use saturated fat like lard, shortening, or animal fat drippings for cooking. Use polyunsaturated oil like corn, safflower, sesame seed, cottonseed, soybean and sunflower oils.

Monounsaturated oils like olive oil and peanut oil are best for your health, according to recent studies. Polyunsaturated oils like corn, safflower, seasame seed, cottonseed, soybean and sunflower oils are better for your coronary health than saturated fat, but not quite as good as monounsaturated oils.

> Eliminate one pie crust when baking pies. Make your pies "open-faced" rather than covering them with a second crust.

• In recipes, reduce the amount of added fat by one-third to one-half. Make up the difference by adding water. For example, if a recipe calls for one cup of oil, just add 2/3 cup of oil and 1/3 cup water. The next time you make the same recipe, try further reducing the amount of oil. Keep cutting back on the fat until you have reached the "lowest possible" fat level for that recipe.

> For sautéing, use a vegetable spray. The spray will limit the amount of fat you'll use in cooking.

> Avoid butter or sour cream on baked potatoes. Eating a plain baked potato is good for you and low in fat!

> Substitute low-fat cottage cheese or nonfat yogurt for sour cream in your favorite recipes.

> Reduce the amount of peanut butter in your diet or eliminate it entirely.

> Eliminate potato chips, french fries and all fried "fast food" from your diet. When eating out, pull off all the crisp, breaded portions from fried foods because they become saturated with cooking oil.

> Eliminating salt and butter or oil on popcorn is not always easy because without the liquid, it seems as if no other herbs or spices will stick to the popcorn. Try this delicious alternative. Lightly spray the popcorn with a "non-stick" vegetable spray, then add cinnamon, curry powder, onion powder (not onion salt), chili powder or other herbs for an enjoyable flavor without cholesterol or salt.

> If you want cheese, eat the low-fat varieties like Mozzarella, Provolone and Swiss.

For the taste of cheese, try a sprinkle of grated Parmesan cheese. It will still give you a cheese flavor but it contains fewer grams of fat.

> Avoid heavy salad dressings like blue cheese. Try to eat less salad dressing by placing the dressing on the side and using it

only as necessary.

> Drink skim or low-fat milk. Avoid using whole milk, evaporated milk, or sweetened, condensed milk. If you want the convenience of condensed milk, use a low-fat evaporated milk powder.

> Switch from ice cream to ice milk, sherbet, sorbet or frozen fruit treats. Beware of frozen yogurt, unless it is frozen low-fat yogurt.

> Limit your intake of baking chocolate or milk chocolate which contains highly saturated cocoa butter. Substitute cocoa powder for chocolate when possible in recipes. The American Heart Association recommends substituting three tablespoons cocoa powder and one tablespoon polyunsaturated oil for each one ounce piece of baking chocolate. It will cut the amount of saturated fat by over 60%.

> Try scallops. They are a low-fat and low-cholesterol seafood.

> Walnuts and pecans are high in polyunsaturates and therefore help to lower blood cholesterol. Chestnuts are also a healthful snack because they are low in fat.

> Avoid all foods prepared with sauces or gravies like a cheese sauce (described as "au gratin"), hollandaise sauce, lobster sauce, sweet and sour sauce, mayonnaise or regular gravy. Tomato sauce may be high in salt!

> When buying processed foods, look for "catch words" on the label that indicate high fat or high cholesterol levels: lard, butter, shortening, fat, cream, hydrogenated or hardened oils, palm, palm kernel oil, coconut oil, whole-milk solids, whole-milk fat, egg solids, egg-yolk solids, suet, animal fat, animal byproducts, cocoa butter, milk chocolate, or imitation milk chocolate. Avoid these products.

> Check food labels very carefully. Products labeled "low-cholesterol" may not conform to the same standards.

> Vitamin C may slow down the formation of certain harmful substances in the body such as "free-radicals". It is thought that free-radicals play a major role in causing hardening of the arteries, heart disease, cancer and aging. Citrus fruit, rose hips, acerola cherries, green peppers, parsley, broccoli, brussels sprouts, cabbage and potatoes are good sources of vitamin C.

> Niacin (vitamin B3) given in high doses has been shown to reduce the amount of cholesterol in the blood (Journal of the American Medical Association JAMA:79). In a study of heart attack victims, it was found that people who took high doses of niacin had an 11 percent lower death rate than those who did not. Niacin must be administered in high doses to be effective in lowering cholesterol. But because of the significant side effects of high doses of niacin, it should be taken only under a doctor's supervision. Some people (those with high blood pressure, diabetes, gout or ulcers) should not take niacin at all. The niacinamide form of the vitamin should not be used because it does not lower blood fats by a significant amount. Food sources for niacin include yeast, fish, poultry, liver, meat, whole-grain products (except corn which contains an inactive form of niacin), peanuts, potatoes, beans and mushrooms.

> High quantities of lecithin combined with a low-saturated fat, low-cholesterol diet may help to lower cholesterol levels more than diet alone, according to Ronald K. Tompkins, M.D. (American Journal of Surgery 140:3). In Dr. Tompkins' study, each person received 48 grams of lecithin a day while maintaining a low-fat diet. Lecithin is a natural source of the vitamin choline which is found in high amounts in soybeans, eggs, fish, liver and wheat germ.

> Love may be an important ingredient in the battle against cholesterol. According to a study by Fred Cornhill at Ohio State University, cholesterol levels were lower in rabbits who had been petted and cuddled daily, than in rabbits who had not received any special attention. The study, reported in Rodale's Natural Healing, noted that in identical circumstances with an identical diet, the animals who received the "tender loving care" had lower cholesterol levels.

Circulation Problems

• Circulation problems are quite common among the elderly and should be evaluated by a physician.

• Vitamin E has an anticoagulant ("anti-clotting") effect that may help prevent certain circulation problems. It has been used to treat intermittent claudication, a condition in which poor circulation in the legs causes leg cramps and may allow blood clots to form.

•   Niacin (vitamin B3) is a vasodilator or blood-vessel enlarger. It may improve circulation in the elderly and help keep the arms and legs from falling asleep. The overall effectiveness of this use of niacin is unknown, and it may vary from person to person.

•   In diabetics, chromium supplements may aid in treating the tendency to have circulation problems.

•   PLEASE NOTE: any vitamin or mineral supplement in amounts beyond the Recommended Daily Allowance (RDA) should only be taken with a physician's approval.

Cold Sensitivity

•   According to the National Institute on Aging, over 2.5 million older Americans are especially vulnerable to cold sensitivity. The U.S. Government reports that people who are at high risk for suffering from hypothermia (low body heat) include:

>   the elderly who are frail or sick
>   the very old
>   people who live alone or in an isolated area
>   the poor (who can't afford adequate heat)
>   the homeless
>   people who do not shiver or feel the cold
>   people on prescription drugs that make them insensitive to cold — antidepressants, blood-pressure reducers, sedatives, tranquilizers and certain heart drugs
>   people who have kidney problems, overactive thyroids or hypoglycemia
>   alcoholics or people who drink a lot of alcohol

•   People at high risk for hypothermia should take precautions to stay warm when it's cold.

>   Wear loose layers of warm clothing when inside or outside. Wearing layers of clothes will make it easier for you to stay comfortable by adding or removing clothing.

>   Do not wear tight clothing or tight jewelry because it can constrict the flow of blood in the body.

>   If your hands or feet are cold, add more clothes to your whole body. Use the temperature of your extremities as a guide to

your whole body's temperature.

> Use an electric blanket or extra blankets when sleeping.

> If feeling cold is a problem while you are sleeping, consider wearing "long johns," comfortable (not tight) socks and a cap to bed.

> People in wheelchairs should consider a "lap blanket" to keep their legs warm.

> After a bath or shower, dry your body and your hair completely to prevent heat loss through evaporation.

> Get enough sleep and rest. If you are tired, your sensitivity to the cold is increased.

> Drink plenty of fluids, but avoid alcohol. Drinking alcohol in cold weather is dangerous because it hinders temperature regulation, according to studies at the University of Southern California's School of Pharmacy. Alcohol can cause a severe loss of body temperature and possibly lead to death.

> Do not smoke or use any nicotine-containing product because nicotine constricts your arteries and makes it hard to keep your hands and feet warm.

> Eat a well-balanced diet.

> When outside, wear a hat and scarf. Up to half of your body heat can be lost through an unprotected head and neck.

> Cover your ears. Use a hat with "ear flaps" or warm ear muffs.

> Keep dry. Remove wet or damp clothing promptly.

> Wear mittens instead of gloves to keep your hands warmer.

> Wear lined boots that cover the calves of the legs. If you don't own boots, wear shoes that are a little large and wear two pairs of socks.

> To avoid inhaling cold air, place a scarf or mask over your nose and mouth. This will help warm the air before it reaches your lungs. The material may get damp if you are outside for a long time, so have an extra dry scarf available.

> Don't go outside on cold, windy days since the wind-chill factor may be much lower than the temperature alone.

> If you are living alone, arrange to have someone come and visit you everyday. An accident could prevent you from being able to stay warm, and a daily visit would provide an opportunity to

reduce the amount of time you would be overexposed to cold.

> Have your home thoroughly insulated including the attic, ceilings, basement and windows. You may also cover your windows or install storm windows (especially on the north side) to reduce drafts in the winter.

> If finances are a problem, consider heating only one or two rooms of your house. But make sure that you will be satisfied to live ONLY in those rooms throughout the winter. Keep the rest of the house warm enough to keep pipes from freezing.

> Low-income families may be able to get special aid from local or state governments in order to keep their homes warm enough throughout the cold months.

> If poor nutrition is a problem, contact a local agency. They may be able to provide a hot meal service that gives shut-ins regular hot, nutritious meals served in their own homes.

> Vitamin C supplementation may help to reduce sensitivity to cold temperatures. Magnesium supplements may aid in adaptation to the cold.

> To improve circulation and avoid getting too cold, elderly people should also get some simple exercise every day. Whether it is walking a short distance or rocking in a rocking chair, physical activity is needed to help keep circulation flowing and maintain good body heat. Dr. Arthur Helfand of the Medical Center in Philadelphia says a rocking chair can provide as much exercise as walking. It uses important muscles in the legs and feet and improves circulation. Almost anyone can rock in a rocking chair.

• Cold feet may be a result of poor circulation caused by clogged arteries, heart problems, or stress. Many people with diabetes, rheumatoid arthritis, collagen disease or lupus suffer from cold feet. Smokers often get cold feet because nicotine constricts the arteries and causes poor circulation. If you suspect your cold feet are related to a circulation problem, you should discuss it with your doctor.

> A warm or hot bath will raise body temperature and warm up the feet. If a bath is not practical, soak your feet in warm water. Placing a hot water bottle or an electric heating pad on the feet may also help. Do not get the water bottle or heating pad too hot because feet with poor circulation might not be sensitive to heat, and you could burn yourself very easily.

> Of course, wearing heavy socks or slippers is an easy way to keep the feet warm. Many people wear socks to bed because even blankets and comforters do not seem to keep their feet warm enough. Placing a blanket, quilt or afghan over the legs and feet while sitting is also effective. Many nursing home residents and people confined to a bed or a wheel-chair use "lap quilts" to help keep their legs and feet comfortable.

• If a person is at high risk, be sure to watch him carefully for clues to his body temperature. Stiff muscles, shivering, trembling, a puffy or bloated face, difficult coordination, slow heart rate, slow breathing, low blood pressure, cool or pale skin, a change in personality and confusion can be caused by a drop in body temperature. Many older people have lost their ability to shiver, so don't just rely on shivering as the main sign of hypothermia.

• If you suspect someone is suffering from overexposure to cold, call an ambulance or a doctor immediately. If a person's temperature drops below 95° F, it is considered to be an emergency. Cover him with blankets, pillows, extra clothes, towels or whatever is available. However, do not move him because he may be very weak. Do not try to "rewarm" him. Don't give him anything to eat or drink. Do not raise the feet because cold blood from the feet will return to the heart and further lower the temperature of the entire body.

Confusion

Mental confusion may be caused by advancing age, serious illness, or by a prolonged deficiency of thiamine (vitamin B1), vitamin B12, folic acid or magnesium.

Mental confusion may also be a side effect of taking certain prescription drugs. If you are taking medication, you may want to discuss your problems with your doctor, who may be able to provide an alternate medicine for you.

Constipation

• Constipation is most often caused by a lack of fiber in the diet. It's especially a problem as we get older. High-fiber diets were normal until modern times. Our digestive systems are designed to handle a diet which contains bran, the outer fiber coat of cereal grains. Modern food processing methods remove most fiber from our food, and this leads to constipation. Fiber, or roughage, absorbs a good deal more than its own weight in water; so this "roughage" really becomes "smoothage" in the intestines.

• You may think that you aren't constipated if you have a bowel movement every day or so. Medically speaking, constipation refers to a hard, dry stool which is difficult to pass. If you consume a low-fiber diet you probably do suffer from some degree of constipation. People who eat enough high-fiber food typically pass (without straining) soft, light brown stools, which have little odor. Their bowel movements are regular, about once a day or more. Their breath is sweet since there isn't much absorption of noxious gas through the intestines into the bloodstream, which is then ventilated through the lungs in constipated people.

• The National Institutes of Health says that each person requires a slightly different bowel schedule — once a day is normal for some people but three times a week might be normal for another person. So "regularity" is different for different people. Regularity should be able to be achieved by completely natural methods:

> Eat plenty of whole grain cereals, rye crackers, bran, bread and flours made with whole grains.

> Eat plenty of fresh fruit.

> Eat plenty of unprocessed foods.

> Eat plenty of fresh vegetables. People who wish to maintain a high level of fiber in their diets should not peel their fruits and vegetables. Much of the fiber content of these foods is in their peels. Legumes are the vegetables with the best source of fiber. Legumes include peanuts, peas and beans. Vegetables that are from the root of the plant, like carrots and potatoes, are also good sources of natural fiber.

> Switch from white rice to brown rice to increase fiber content.

> Drink more water. Water is the safest and **most effective** laxative. Dietary fiber absorbs water and swells to provide natural bulk in the digestive tract. Adults should drink eight glasses of

water (two quarts) each day. According to research on constipation by Lederle Laboratories, feces are 75 percent water. Hard feces found in constipation contain less water. A person must drink plenty of fluids each day to help in the excretion of soft stools.

> Cut back on the amount of hot and cold tea you drink. According to the British Medical Journal (3/14/81), excessive tea drinking can cause constipation and colon cancer probably as a result of cancer causing tannins found in tea. If you are a tea drinker and experience **any** anal irritation or constriction quit before it's too late and cancer sets in.

• Coffee may help with regularity, according to a study by researchers at the University of Kansas College of Health Sciences and Hospital. The researchers tested what many of their patients had claimed for years: without their coffee in the morning, they just couldn't "get going." They discovered that 2-1/2 cups of regular or decaffeinated coffee did produce more frequent and easier bowel movements, compared to drinking other warm beverages or going without coffee. (All the people in the test were placed on identical diets so the amount of fiber in the diet, the best source of regularity, did not affect the study results).

In other research, drinking a cup of hot water about half an hour before breakfast seems to have a mild laxative effect. Maybe this is partially why hot coffee is so effective!

• Get regular exercise. Lack of exercise is a common cause of constipation. Inactivity is one reason why constipation is prevalent among many older people.

• Constipation may be caused by certain prescription and non-prescription drugs. Many prescription drugs like antidepressants, pain relievers containing narcotics, diuretics, and drugs used to treat Parkinson's Disease can cause constipation. Some over-the-counter drugs like laxatives and antacids containing calcium and aluminum can also contribute to the problem of constipation. Paradoxically, certain laxatives, especially stimulant laxatives, can cause constipation in the long run because the body builds up a tolerance to them after long-term use.

• Avoid using commercial laxatives. Frequent use of laxatives can cause constipation because laxatives make the body's natural bowel mechanisms insensitive. Using commercial laxatives may cause you to become dependent on the laxatives as your own system will eventually lose its natural abilities. Mineral oil should not be used as a laxative because, if even a very small amount gets into the lungs, it can cause a serious form of pneumonia. Also, mineral oil can lead to a deficiency of some vitamins, including vitamins A, D, E and K, reports <u>Pharmacy Times</u>. Mineral oil doesn't allow the body to properly absorb these vitamins from food.

- Do not use laxatives if:
> you experience nausea or vomiting
> appendicitis is suspected
> you experience abdominal pain
> the intestine could be obstructed or damaged

- For many years, prunes have been recommended as natural laxatives, presumably only because they are a good source of fiber. However, scientists have recently discovered that a natural laxative called diphenylisatin is found in them.

- Physical or emotional stress can also add to constipation problems. During pregnancy, while traveling or under other times of severe stress, be especially careful to eat plenty of fiber and drink lots of fluids.

- Avoid all straining during bowel movements. Take time for your bowel movements. Straining during a bowel movement may cause hemorrhoids, varicose veins and bowel problems. High-fiber diets help people avoid straining at stool.

- If you suffer from prolonged constipation lasting over a week, see your doctor. Extended constipation could be a sign of a more serious illness, like cancer of the colon, irritable bowel syndrome or diverticular disease in the colon.

Corns or Calluses
- Corns are the most common foot problem in older Americans. Corns usually appear on the toes. They are caused by undue pressure or friction, usually from improperly-fitting shoes. They form at a point where friction or pressure causes the blood supply to that area to be increased. This causes the skin cells there to grow rapidly, and an overgrowth of cells occurs.
- Calluses are usually flat and wide. Corns are usually

cone-shaped. Corns are more painful than calluses, even though both are dead skin. Corns have a central core, and pressure from the foot is concentrated with great force in this small area. The larger the corn, the more likely it will be painful when external pressure or friction occurs!

•   The first step to prevent corns and calluses is to wear only shoes or sandals that do not constrict your toes or feet. Wear shoes that have less than two-inch heels so you don't put extra pressure on your toes. If necessary, have your shoes widened or stretched by a shoe-repairer. Discard or give away any shoes that do not fit you comfortably and properly.

•   Once a corn or callus appears, you can help relieve the soreness by wearing moleskin around the corn or using a hole-in-the-center corn pad. This will take the pressure off the corn and should help relieve any pain.

•   When removing the corn or callus, ONLY the DEAD layers of skin should be taken off. Soak your foot in hot water or castor oil for at least 15 minutes. Then gently scrub the dead skin away with an emery board, rough towel or a pumice stone. Scrub off only dead skin and never use a razor or knife to cut off the skin! Stop scrubbing if the area around the corn or callus appears red. Repeat this procedure at least twice a week. Unfortunately, the corn or callus will come back if you don't change your shoes or relieve the pressure that originally created the corn or callus.

•   A mixture of aspirin, lemon juice and water is "the" solution for calluses on your feet, according to Dr. Suzanne M. Levine, author of My Feet Are Killing Me. Dr. Levine recommends crushing six aspirin into a powder and mixing them with one tablespoon of lemon juice and one tablespoon of water. Rub the paste onto the problem area on your foot. Then, wrap your foot in a plastic bag and a towel to create a warm, moist atmosphere so the paste can penetrate the hard calluses. After 15 minutes, unwrap your foot and gently use a pumice stone to wipe away the hard, dead skin. You may need to repeat this procedure a few times before all of the hard spots are removed.

If you have diabetes or a circulation problem, you should discuss your corns and calluses with a doctor because home treatment could be dangerous for you.

Depression

Prescription drugs, including blood-pressure reducers, sleeping pills, and tranquilizers frequently cause depression as a side effect.

Overdoses of certain vitamins, especially niacinamide, can cause depression.

Vitamin deficiencies, especially deficiencies of B vitamins, can cause depression. Depression is an early symptom of thiamine (vitamin B1), riboflavin (vitamin B2), niacin (vitamin B3), pyridoxine (vitamin B6) and vitamin B12 deficiency. Depression can be a signal of advanced deficiency of vitamin C.

According to the Recommended Daily Dietary Allowance, (RDA) adults need 1.0 - 1.5 mg. of thiamine, 1.2 - 1.7 mg. of riboflavin, 13 - 18 mg. of niacin, 1.2 - 2.2 mg. of pyridoxine and 3.0 mcg. of vitamin B12 each day.

Pantothenic acid (vitamin B5) has been reported to improve symptoms of senility and depression when taken with other B vitamins.

Allergies to foods, like corn or gluten, can cause depression, especially if the allergy causes intestinal problems which interfere with the absorption of vitamins.

Eating foods containing large amounts of sugar or flour may cause low blood sugar levels and depression.

Alcohol causes mental depression. Withdrawal from drugs, including caffeine, nicotine and alcohol, may cause depression.

Bright indoor lighting helps some people fight depression in the winter by stimulating the brain and the pineal gland. Vigorous exercise for a few minutes a day stimulates the brain and may also help combat depression.

Diabetes

• As you get older, your hormone levels naturally drop off. Obesity and unnatural eating habits put too much strain on your body, and you may become prone to maturity-onset diabetes. However, some cases of diabetes aren't caused by diet or obesity. In juvenile diabetes there is a lack of insulin, possibly caused by a viral attack on the insulin-producing cells. Juvenile diabetes, usually, but not always, strikes early in life.

• A high-fiber diet during your lifetime may reduce your chances of getting diabetes later in life. Diets which aren't low in fat or high in fiber contribute to obesity and make it difficult for insulin to be properly utilized. However, if you already have diabetes, be sure to check with your doctor before you go on a high-fiber diet. Your doctor may have you on medication, and any change in your diet can upset the carefully balanced carbohydrate requirements that have been established for you.

• Studies have shown that the mineral chromium can even-out swings in blood sugar levels in people who have a tendency toward low blood sugar (hypoglycemia) or high blood sugar. Chromium supplements may aid in the treatment of maturity-onset diabetes and problems which are associated with diabetes, such as a tendency towards infections, heart and circulatory problems. Adults need between 50 - 200 mcg. of chromium per day.

• Studies by Kurt A. Oster, M.D. and others indicate that large doses of folic acid (as much as 80 mg. per day, many times the Recommended Daily Allowance) may be helpful in the treatment and prevention of diabetes. Larger, controlled studies are necessary to confirm these initial studies and reports of clinical experience. Large amounts of vitamins should only be taken under a doctor's care.

• People with diabetes are unusually prone to zinc deficiency because diabetes lowers the blood levels of zinc. Adults need 15 mg. of zinc daily.

• Supplementation of the mineral manganese has been reported to cause improvement in some cases of diabetes. The Recommended Daily Dietary Allowance (RDA) of manganese for adults is 2.5 - 5.0 mg. It is deficient in many diets.

• New scientific reports claim that garlic may help in the fight against diabetes.

• Exercise may help improve a person's sensitivity to insulin, according to a study in the Journal of the American Medical Association (JAMA 252: 645). Many diabetics over 60 years of age seem to lose their responsiveness to insulin treatment. As the insulin seems to lose its effectiveness, the incidence of heart and artery problems increases. A study at the Washington University School of Medicine in St. Louis showed that people over 60 who participated in regular exercise did not experience a lower response to the insulin. When exercise programs were started for diabetics over 60 who had already experienced a decrease in the insulin response, their insulin sensitivity greatly improved. To retain sensitivity to insulin, older diabetics should exercise for at least 45 minutes, three times each week. The exercise could be walking, jogging, cycling, or using a treadmill. The researchers reported that more strenuous activity improved the response better than less strenuous exercise.

CAUTION! Your physician should be consulted before beginning any new physical activities. An increase in physical activity can dangerously lower the blood sugar levels of a diabetic who has taken insulin, thus greatly increasing the likelihood of insulin shock. Your doctor can help outline a program suited to your needs that will begin with less strenuous exercises and gradually increase to more difficult ones.

• Massaging the site of an insulin injection can help get more of the medicine into a diabetic's system, says Modern Medicine (52:122,43). For diabetics on insulin shots, the researchers recommend massaging the injection site for three minutes after the insulin injection. Dr. Richard S. Dillion of Bryn Mawr Hospital in Pennsylvania reports that more insulin will get into the person's system with this method. In two years of research with 26 diabetics, Dr. Dillion found that massaging improved the ability to maintain consistent blood sugar levels.

• Diabetics often have problems with circulation, so daily attention should be given to the feet. Keep your feet clean and dry; toenails clipped straight across; corns and calluses should be examined by your doctor or podiatrist. Buy shoes that fit well, are comfortable and are made of breathable leather, not plastic or vinyl.

• Diabetics should not take fish oil supplements to lower their cholesterol levels. Harry S. Glauber of the University of California at San Diego reports that fish oil capsules can actually raise blood sugar levels in diabetics. People with inactive diabetes may discover that the fish oils activate the problem, Glauber says. He recommends that diabetics and people at high risk for developing diabetes should avoid the supplements until further research can be done. If a diabetic needs to lower cholesterol, eating cold-water fish like salmon, trout, mackerel and cod will provide plenty of healthful fish oils without having to take commercial supplements.

• Diabetics and people with high blood pressure should avoid overeating when they are on antidepressant drugs. Unusual feelings of hunger and cravings for sweet food are experienced by about 50% of people taking drugs for depression, according to the journal Geriatrics (41:4). The unusual cravings often cause people to eat more than normal and gain weight. Being overweight is dangerous for everyone, but especially for diabetics. The pangs of hunger and cravings for sweets seem to be side effects of antidepressant drugs that stop as soon as the drugs are discontinued, says the report. If you suspect that your prescription drugs are causing these side effects, discuss them with your doctor. Do NOT stop or change your medication without your physician's approval.

• People with diabetes should consult their physicians before taking thiamine (vitamin B1) supplements because large doses of thiamine may inactivate insulin.

• Research has shown that people with diabetes may need extra vitamin C. However, diabetics may not be able to properly metabolize vitamin C. This may contribute to the blood vessel damage that diabetics often experience.

Diabetics taking oral drugs to lower their blood sugar levels should not take vitamin C without the supervision of their physician. Vitamin C may actually block the action of these drugs.

• Research at the Veterans Administration Medical Center in Birmingham, Alabama, has shown that inositol helps eliminate nerve pain associated with severe diabetes. Inositol does not have an official RDA (Recommended Daily Dietary Allowance) set by the U.S. Government. However, inositol is generally recognized to have many vitamin-like qualities and is important in the functioning of the nervous system. The best food sources of inositol are organ meats, yeast, beans, (especially great northern beans), whole-grain products, peanuts, citrus fruits (especially grapefruit or orange juice) and fresh cantaloupe. Caffeine interferes with the body's use of inositol, so don't use any products that contain caffeine. Biotin, choline and vitamin E are needed for inositol to be used most effectively in the body.

Diarrhea

• Diarrhea can be caused by excessive amounts of vitamins, certain prescription drugs, or more commonly by an infection which may be mild or serious. Diarrhea can also be a symptom of a serious intestinal disease. Anyone with diarrhea should consult a physician to make sure that nothing serious is wrong. Persistent diarrhea from an infection or parasite may be treated with drugs. If nothing serious is wrong, several steps may help to minimize or eliminate diarrhea.

> Over-the-counter liquids containing bismuth may be helpful for common diarrhea.

> Avoid taking vitamins or minerals on an empty stomach.

> Check with your doctor to see if diarrhea could be a side effect of your prescription medicine. Many prescription drugs can cause diarrhea including: anti- inflammatories used to treat arthritis, thiazide diuretics used to lower blood pressure, some anticlotting drugs like Coumadin®, some antibiotics like Cleocin™, and Tagamet®, which is used in the treatment of stomach ulcers.

> Milk and dairy products cause diarrhea and bloating in certain people who have difficulty digesting lactose. If lactose intolerance is a problem, you should avoid milk products containing lactose or use a predigested type of milk to which the enzyme lactase has been added.

• Some diarrhea, unexplained gas and bloating is caused by the artificial sweetener sorbitol. "Excess consumption of sorbitol may have a laxative effect," according to the Food and Drug Administration (FDA). Sorbitol is found in many kinds of food products, including ice cream, gum, carbonated drinks, jelly and baked goods. It is also found naturally in some fruits, like prunes. If you consume a lot of sorbitol-containing products and are suffering from diarrhea or unexplained gas, try reading labels for listed ingredients and eliminating sorbitol from your diet.

• Diarrhea may cause dehydration and chemical imbalances in the body. Serious fluid loss may have to be treated in a hospital with intravenous therapy. Moderate fluid loss can be treated under a physician's guidance at home by taking plenty of liquids plus moderate amounts of potassium chloride, which is found in some brands of "light" salt, and sodium bicarbonate.

• When treating diarrhea or an upset stomach with clear liquids, the temperature of the liquid is just as important as the type of liquid. Cold liquids tend to stimulate the intestines and make diarrhea worse. Drinks that are at room temperature or slightly warm are the best for diarrhea or stomach indigestion.

• Vitamin C in the form of ascorbic acid can cause nausea, indigestion and diarrhea. Ascorbic acid should always be taken with food or with a large amount of water and an antacid to help minimize these effects.

Diverticular Disease

Diverticular disease is the out-ballooning of areas of the intestine into little pockets, diverticuli, in which fecal matter can lodge and cause infection. It occurs mostly in the elderly. Many doctors who treat people with diverticular disease now recommend that they eat a diet high in dietary fiber or take a fiber supplement. The types of fiber recommended are the mushy types such as psyllium seed products or oat bran, as well as whole grain products. Hard types of fiber such as popcorn should be avoided.

People with diverticulosis or diverticulitis (an active infection of diverticuli) experience far fewer relapses if they consume appropriate dietary fiber daily, than if they eat a diet like the traditional American diet which is quite low in dietary fiber. Although the problems caused by diverticular disease will not disappear on a high fiber diet or after taking a fiber supplement daily, in most cases they can be minimized and controlled so that surgery or antibiotic treatment can be avoided.

Dizziness

• Frequent dizzy spells should be reported to your doctor as soon as possible. If you are taking a lot of aspirin or any other drugs, be sure to tell the doctor about all the medication you are taking, including all over-the-counter drugs, because the medication may be the reason for the dizziness. (Geriatrics 41: 7, 31). Many times dizziness is just a side effect of aspirin or another drug, especially drugs taken to control blood pressure. Since aspirin is so commonly used, we sometimes forget that it is a drug and can cause serious side effects.

• Dizziness can lead to dangerous falls or accidents while driving. Walk or travel with utmost caution.

Dowager's Hump — See Osteoporosis.

Dry Mouth
• Saliva helps to break down food particles, cleanse the teeth, prevent tooth decay and stimulate the taste buds, according to the National Institute of Dental Research. Therefore, it is important to treat a dry mouth to prevent dental problems.

• Thirst and dryness of the mouth can be caused by an overdose of calcium or vitamin D, or by a deficiency of potassium. A severe deficiency of sodium chloride (salt) can also cause dehydration.

• Severe dry mouth may be a symptom of a serious disease or a side effect of a drug. There are many drugs that can cause dry mouth, including these commonly prescribed medications: Aldactone®, Aldomet®, Artane®, Benadryl®, Bentyl®, Catapres®, Cogentin®, Combid®, Dimetapp®, Donnatal®, Ditropan®, Elavil®, Flexeril®, HydroDIURIL®, Lasix®, Lomotil®, Mellaril®, Minipress®, nitroglycerin taken in pill form, Ornade®, Symmetrel®, Tenuate®, Triavil®, Valium®, many antihistamines, and most antidepressants.

• Make sure you are drinking at least eight glasses (2 quarts) of water a day as the first treatment of thirst and dry mouth.

• People suffering from dry mouth should avoid cigarettes, alcohol and spicy, salty or highly acidic foods. Over-the-counter artificial salivas, Xero- Lube® and Moi-Stir®, can be used to help relieve dry mouth problems.

Emphysema   See: Lung Diseases

Eye Problems

- Protecting our eyes is important if we hope to keep our eyesight throughout our lives. Here are several easy steps for prevention recommended by The National Society to Prevent Blindness. To avoid loss of your eyesight:

> Have frequent eye check-ups if you have high blood pressure, diabetes or a history of vision problems.

> Pain in the eyes, excessive discharge from the eyes, loss of vision, dry eyes, double vision, and swelling or redness of the eye or eyelid are possible warning signs of vision problems and should be checked immediately by an eye doctor.

> Even if you do not experience any loss of vision, you should have a regular eye exam by an ophthalmologist at least once every two years, so that possible problems can be detected early.

> Don't rub your eye if you get a speck in it. Lift the upper eyelid outward and down over the lower lid, and let the tears wash out the speck or particle.

- Reduced vision in the elderly is sometimes related to poor lighting in their homes, according to an article in The Lancet journal. Researchers at London's St. Bartholomew's Hospital discovered that many elderly people used only one-tenth of the light used in the hospital. When the elderly people added a small light with a 60-watt bulb to illuminate their homes, vision improved in 82% of the patients. Before loss of vision in the elderly is assumed to be permanent, home lighting should be checked.

Use adequate lighting for all demanding visual tasks like reading, watching TV, cooking and handicrafts. Use regular lightbulbs (incandescent light) instead of tubular overhead lights (fluorescent light). Incandescent light is easier on the eyes. Try to avoid straining the eyes.

- Itching, burning eyes, night blindness or loss of vision in near darkness are some of the early symptoms of vitamin A deficiency. Vitamin A can naturally be obtained in liver, cod liver oil, eggs, whole milk products, broccoli, spinach, and other green leafy vegetables. Carotene, which a healthy body can convert into vitamin A, is found in yellow fruits and vegetables, like carrots.

- Wear sunglasses that block ultraviolet light and transmit no more than 30 percent of light to the eyes. Ultraviolet rays can damage the eyes and increase your chances of developing cataracts or eye cancer. According to the New England Journal of Medicine (13: 313) a deadly cancer of the eye, called intraocular malignant melanoma, is mostly likely to occur in people who have spent a lot of time outdoors, sun bathers or those who use sun lamps. You can lower your risk by wearing protective sun glasses, hats, or visors while in the sun. Sitting under an umbrella at the beach may protect you from direct sunlight, but some of the dangerous rays bounce off the sand and back under the umbrella. Even under an umbrella, you should still protect your eyes and wear a sunscreen to protect your skin. Being on sand, snow or a large body of water will increase your exposure to ultraviolet rays if you are not protected.

• Never look directly into the sun. Many people irreversibly damage their eyes by looking at the sun. Just because it is not painful does not mean that staring into the sun is not harmful.

• Don't share any items that touch your eyes. Eye make-up, towels or eye make-up applicators should never be used by more than one person. Throw away old eye make-up since it can easily become contaminated.

• Chronic redness of the eyes may be caused by a lack of tears. Sometimes dry eyes are caused by changes in the hormonal balance in a woman, an environment that is too dry or windy, or over-exposure to the sun. Artificial tears, available over-the-counter, may help. Sleeping with a bedroom humidifier, protecting the eyes with wrap-around sunglasses and avoiding exposure to wind, sun or dirty air may help reduce dryness.

Falls

• Falls are the single most common cause of accidental death in people aged 65 and older. Falls also cause hip fractures which can immobilize an elderly person and lead to blood clots and other complications. Many accidental falls by the elderly may be caused by medication, according to an extensive study by a California pharmacist. In a fourteen-month study, Kerry G. Sobel, Pharm. D. of Northwestern Memorial Hospital, found that several specific drug classes are associated with falls in elderly patients in nursing homes. People taking diuretics, sedatives and sleeping pills are at an increased risk of suffering a disabling fall.

• Another recent study in The New England Journal Of Medicine (316:7,363-9) found several other drugs that caused an increased risk of hip fractures. Drugs which are slowly excreted by the body were discovered to cause the most falls. Because there is difficulty in passing drugs through the bodies of elderly people, "slow moving" drugs become more harmful, says the report. Most of these medications are mood-altering drugs used in the treatment of depression, insomnia, anxiety, or psychosis:

> amitriptyline (Elavil®, Triavil®)

> chlordiazepoxide (Librium®, Librax®)

> chlorpromazine (Thorazine®)

> diazepam (Valium®)

> doxepin (Adapin®, Sinequan®)

> haloperidol (Haldol®)

> imipramine (Tofranil®)

> thioridazine (Mellaril®)

• To help prevent accidental falls:

> Avoid using "scatter" rugs in the home. If they are used, tape them to the floor. Make sure that the edges of all rugs, carpets and flooring are securely fastened to the floor.

> Use a bench in your bathtub or shower so you can sit and shower. Install grab bars in your shower or over your tub. Use adhesive rubber strips to prevent slipping because rubber mats can slide.

> Put adhesive rubber strips on stairs.

> Use handrails whenever possible. Have handrails built for all steps and ramps in your home if you can afford it.

> Put wires and cables behind or under furniture where they will be out of the way. (Don't put electrical wires under carpet or rugs — they'll become a fire hazard.)

> Make sure the inside and the outside of your home are well-lit so you can avoid any obstacles.

> Avoid the use of alcohol. It is another drug that can contribute to dangerous falls.

Fatigue   see: **Tiredness**

Feeling — Loss of
•   Feeling loss or numbness may be a symptom of a serious disease which needs medical treatment.

•   Loss of feeling combined with tingling or burning sensations may be a symptom of a lack of thiamine (vitamin B1).

•   A deficiency of vitamin B12 can also lead to numbness and tingling of the feet.

•   Niacin (vitamin B3) may improve circulation in the elderly thus keeping arms and legs from falling asleep. The overall effectiveness of this use of niacin is unknown, and it may vary from person to person.

•   Very large doses of vitamin B6, pyridoxine, may cause nerve damage and loss of feeling in the arms and legs. Most feeling usually returns when people stop taking too much of the vitamin.

Fluid Retention
•   Fluid retention is the excessive accumulation of fluid in the body tissues, medically referred to as edema or dropsy. Fluid retention can be the result of an inflammation or an illness like congestive heart disease, so be sure to check with your doctor to see if medical treatment is necessary.

•   Some women suffer from a weight gain of up to five pounds of fluid, particularly just prior to menstruation. Pyridoxine (vitamin B6) supplements may help relieve or reduce the symptoms of pre-menstrual fluid retention, weight gain, pre-menstrual acne, depression and menopausal arthritis. Serious side effects have been reported after taking more than 25 mg. of vitamin B6 daily.

•   Potassium supplements are claimed to help reduce fluid retention, but be careful not to exceed the daily dose recommendations for potassium.

•   Prolonged deficiency of thiamine (vitamin B1) can lead to fluid retention and swelling in the hands and feet.

•   To prevent excess fluid retention:
>   Exercise regularly.

> Lose weight.

> Avoid salt.

> Rest your legs and feet at least twice a day by lying with your feet higher than your heart.

> Wear support panty-hose when possible.

> Avoid eating black licorice or licorice extracts because they may contribute to salt and fluid retention. About 90% of the licorice imported into the United States is used in chewing tobacco. This is another reason people should avoid all forms of tobacco use.

Foot Problems

• Diabetics and elderly people with circulation problems or nerve damage in the feet are especially prone to foot problems. Amputation may be necessary if sores in such people aren't treated quickly. Here are some tips on good foot care from Women's Day magazine (49:13) and the Better Health newsletter (10/86):

> Wash your feet daily, but do not soak them for long periods of time. Soaking may cause them to dry out. If you shower, you should wash your feet separately, in a basin of warm, sudsy water. If you have nerve damage in your feet, be sure to check the water temperature before you put your feet into the basin or tub.

> Dry your feet carefully. Be gentle, yet thorough.

> If you have problems with foot odor, excessive perspiring of the feet, or fungus growth on the feet, you may want to sprinkle medicated or unmedicated talcum powder on your feet after drying them. Powder between the toes and on the soles of your feet is best. Use as little powder as possible. If the powder clumps, you have used too much.

> If you have problems with dry skin on your feet, you may want to moisturize them at least once a week. Use a water-based moisturizer or petroleum jelly. To avoid possible fungus infections, don't put moisturizer around your toenails or between your toes. Apply the moisturizer just before going to bed and put on a pair of socks. The socks will keep the moisturizer on your feet and not on the bed linens.

> Inspect your feet daily if you are in a high risk category for serious foot problems. Let your doctor know if you develop an ingrown toenail, blister, bunion, bruise or a sore that seems slow to heal.

People at high risk should not use harsh preparations to treat their foot problems. Gentle massaging with a soft washcloth is acceptable. See your doctor or podiatrist (a foot specialist) as soon as possible when problems occur.

> Never break or lance a blister. Don't tear off any "loose" skin. You should cleanse the area including the loose skin. Clean, loose skin serves as a natural bandage. It will protect the problem area from infection and help speed the healing process.

> A mixture of aspirin, lemon juice and water is the solution for calluses on your feet, according to Dr. Suzanne M. Levine, author of My Feet Are Killing Me. Dr. Levine recommends crushing six aspirin into a powder and mixing them with one tablespoon of lemon juice and one tablespoon of water. Rub the paste onto the problem area on your foot. Then, wrap your foot in a plastic bag and a towel to create a warm, moist atmosphere so the paste can penetrate the hard calluses. After 15 minutes, unwrap your foot and gently use a pumice stone to wipe away the hard, dead skin. You may need to repeat this procedure a few times before all of the hard spots are removed. Also, you may need to change the shoes that caused the calluses.

> Trim or file your toenails straight across. Curving the nail will increase the incidence of ingrown toenails.

> Don't cut your toenails shorter than the end of the toe. The shorter the nail is cut, the more chance of developing an ingrown toenail.

> Using an emery board, file each nail until it is smooth.

> Buy and wear shoes that fit properly. If the shoes do not fit properly in the store, do not allow the salesman to "stretch" them or alter them. Don't buy them if they don't fit the first time you put them on.

> Buy shoes in the afternoon or evening to get a proper fit. During the day your feet swell slightly. If you buy your shoes in the morning, your feet may be smaller than usual and the shoes will not fit later.

> Buy shoes that give your toes plenty of breathing room.

There should be at least a quarter of an inch between your longest toe and the shoe. Avoid pointed shoes because they don't give your toes enough room.

> If you suffer from ingrown toenails, you should not buy sandals or shoes without a toe cover. Ingrown toenails can be aggravated if they are banged or stubbed. Be sure to wear shoes that will protect your toes and toenails.

> Wear high heels as little as possible. They are acceptable for short periods of time, but do not wear them if you must do a lot of standing or walking.

> Buy shoes that are made of natural materials or fabrics. Vinyl, plastic and other man-made materials will not allow the feet to breathe. Without proper ventilation, infections, blisters and foot odor can flourish.

> If you are elderly or have difficulty walking, try to buy shoes with soles that grip the floor. Many soles have special ridges in them to help reduce slipping and falling.

> For the best support and comfort, buy shoes with flexible soles that will cushion your feet.

> When you buy a new pair of shoes, break them in slowly. If you are buying shoes for a specific event, try to buy them at least two weeks early. Wear the shoes around the house for one hour each day. Breaking shoes in gradually will help prevent blisters and soreness from occurring.

> Keep your shoes in good repair. Don't allow the heels to get worn or the soles to wear unevenly.

> Do not wear slippers when you need the support of a pair of shoes.

> If you suffer from dry, cracked feet, DO NOT go barefoot. Going barefoot is good only on soft surfaces like sand, grass and soft dirt. Do not go barefoot for long periods of time in your own home. Without any protection, your feet could lose natural oils and be damaged.

> Don't wear socks that have seams or darning in them. These irregular surfaces may cause blisters or irritation of the feet.

> Natural fibers like cotton and wool are better than socks made from synthetic materials which don't absorb perspiration well.

> Wear clean socks. If your feet perspire a lot, change your

socks twice a day.

> Don't wear socks that are tight at the top. Many socks have an elastic band that holds up the socks but cuts off the circulation!

Gallstones

• Gallstones are common in all western countries for which there are available statistics. Gallstones affect every social class, and there is an increasing incidence among younger people. Gallstone formation formerly had been regarded as a disease of the middle-aged and elderly. Women are about twice as prone as men to form gallstones.

Studies done by Pomare and Heaton in 1973 and 1974 suggest that a high-fiber diet may lessen the risk of gallstone formation. The addition of bran to the diet seemed to interfere with the appearance of a secondary bile salt which makes the bile more saturated with cholesterol and keeps cholesterol from being secreted into the intestine. Since almost all gallstones in the people of western countries consist of cholesterol, this research has important implications in the prevention of gallstone formation.

There is increasing evidence that eating whole grain foods and bran, plus avoiding high-fat diets, should be helpful in the prevention of gallstone formation.

• Lecithin, a substance extracted from egg yolks, soybeans and other high-fat foods, is thought to be important to keep liver cell membranes healthy and perhaps reduce the chance of getting gallstones, according to Tim Watkins of the City University of New York. The manufacturer of Lipton® soup is reported to be hoping to capitalize on this study by selling a new "healthy" soup containing a high percentage of pure lecithin.

• According to researchers at Flinders Medical Center in Australia, one ounce of alcohol per day reduced the risk of developing gallstones. Studies show that high amounts of sugar, alcohol, and fat increase the risk of getting gallstones, but this study showed that just a small amount of alcohol each day actually decreased the risk factor.

• Dr. Heaton of England's Bristol University recommends a low-calorie diet with special emphasis upon a restricted intake of refined carbohydrates (sugar and white flour) to prevent gallstones. The British Medical Journal reports that vegetarians are less likely to suffer from gallstones than non-vegetarians.

• If you already have gallstones, you may be able to avoid a gallbladder operation through one of the experimental methods now being investigated. One new method of crushing gallstones without surgery is to use a lithotripser. A lithotripser uses "sound waves" to painlessly break up and crush kidney stones in the body. Although the use of the lithotripser for crushing gallstones is new and experimental, this use may become more widespread in the future if certain difficulties can be overcome. Many major medical centers now have lithotripsers.

A natural remedy is two weeks on a balanced diet, followed by three days on fruit juice, then half a pint of olive oil and half a pint of lemon juice once a day, with only water to drink the rest of the time. The oil seems to help the gallstones pass naturally. We can't confirm how safe or successful this treatment night be or if there are side effects, so don't try it unless your doctor wants you to.

Other promising techniques of avoiding gallbladder operations involve administering certain drugs, often directly to the gallbladder through a catheter, which may dissolve the gallstones.

Gas

• Avoid foods known to cause gas. According to The FDA Consumer, these foods cause the most gas problems: beans, bagels, bran, broccoli, brussels sprouts, cabbage, cauliflower, and onions.

Apples, apricots, breads, bananas, carrots, celery, citrus fruits, eggplant, prune juice, radishes, and raisins can cause moderate amounts of gas, reports the FDA. Try eliminating these foods, one by one, to see if you can determine which ones give you problems.

• The FDA Consumer (21:3) reports that "swallowing air" is the most common cause of stomach gas. To lessen the amount of air you swallow, follow these suggestions:

> Eat slowly by putting your knife and fork down between bites. This will slow down your eating and reduce the amount of air you swallow with each bite.

> Don't cnew gum. Chewing gum increases the amount of

air swallowed.

> Have your dentures checked. Dentures that do not fit properly can add to the amount of air you swallow.

> Avoid soft drinks and beer. These beverages contain carbon dioxide which can cause gas within your body.

> Avoid milk and dairy products if you have lactose-intolerance which is the most common cause of colitis with its symptoms of chronic diarrhea and gas. (Lactose is a natural enzyme within the body, necessary for digesting milk).

> Avoid foods with a high fat content because they can slow down the digestive system and create gas build-up.

• The FDA has also tested several folk remedies which they discovered to have "no effect" in relieving gas problems. These include the blessed thistle plant, dehydrated garlic, ox bile, and the roots of the golden seal plant.

• Great stress can also cause gas problems. Try to reduce the stressful factors in your lifestyle.

Glaucoma

Glaucoma is a build-up of fluids and pressure within the eye, which may ultimately lead to blindness. there is a herediatary tendency to develop glaucoma, so regular eye examinations which include glaucoma testing are important. Glaucoma is treated medically with drugs and surgery.

• Glaucoma may be aggravated by taking large doses of vitamin D in the form of supplements, or by heavy exposure to sunlight.

• Large doses of niacin (vitamin B3) may also aggravate glaucoma and increase the chances of getting cataracts.

• Vitamin A, choline and vitamin C supplements may help in the treatment of glaucoma but the effectiveness of such treatment is questionable.

Gout

• Gouty arthritis is a metabolic disorder affecting the body's whole system, not just individual joints. It is caused by an over-accumulation of uric acid in the body. If left untreated, gout can lead to death from kidney disease, high blood pressure or heart disease.

• Gout is the only form of arthritis that, in most cases, can be controlled by a proper diet. At one time, gout was considered to be a disease of the rich. Many wealthy people, who over-indulged in rich food, suffered from gout. However, gout can affect anyone.

• Because it is a metabolic disorder, it usually can be controlled by eating a low purine or purine-free diet. After the first onset of gout, limiting purine intake can usually control future attacks and prevent joint damage. Purines are present in many foods.

> Foods containing high amounts of purine are: anchovies, bacon, beef, brains, calf tongue, carp, chicken soup, cod fish, consommé soup, duck, fish roe, fowl, goose gravy, halibut, heart, herring, kidney (beef), lentils, liver, liver sausage, meat extracts, meat soup, partridge, perch, pheasant, pigeon, pike, pork, quail, rabbit, sardines (in oil), shell fish, sweetbreads, trout, turkey, veal, venison.

> Foods that contain moderate amounts of purine are: asparagus, beans, bluefish, bran, bran flakes, cauliflower, chicken, crab, cracked wheat, eel, fish, graham bread, graham crackers, graham porridge, ham, kidney beans, lima beans, malt breakfast food, mushrooms, mutton, navy beans, oatmeal, oysters, peas, puffed wheat, rolled wheat, rye bread, rye krisp, salmon, shad, shredded wheat, spinach, tripe, tuna fish, wheat cakes, whitefish, wholegrain products.

> All meat, game and fish contain purines. Therefore, any meat should be eaten in small portions.

> Alcohol should be avoided since it aggravates gout.

> Condiments, spices, seasonings of all types, concentrated sweets, rich pastries and fried foods should be restricted in the diet.

> Fats should be limited because they interfere with the removal of uric acid from the body.

> Drink plenty of fluids. Two quarts of fluids each day will help reduce the concentration of uric acid in the blood and help keep uric acid crystals from forming on the joints.

Gum Disease

• Prevention is the best way to fight most gum disease, which causes more loss of teeth than cavities. Gum disease in early stages is called gingivitis. Advanced gum disease is known as periodontitis. Gum disease can lead to the loss of many or all of your teeth, but it can be prevented.

> Brush your teeth and tongue after every meal. Brush immediately after eating sugary candy or dried fruit.

> Use a toothbrush with soft bristles — hard bristles can damage the gums and the enamel on your teeth.

> Use a salt, soda, or salt and soda solution instead of commercial toothpaste, recommends Dr. Paul Keyes at the National Institute of Dental Research. Dr. Keyes also treats gum disease with greater success than surgery by having his patients brush at the gum line with a toothbrush dipped in 1% hydrogen peroxide and baking soda.

> If you use a commercial toothpaste, use a tartar control formula.

> Floss at least once daily.

> Massage your gums by using a Water Pik® or similar device, the rubber tip on the end of some toothbrushes, or special brushing aids.

> Reduce your intake of sugary foods and candies or eliminate them from your diet.

> Have your teeth professionally cleaned at least twice a year.

> Reduce stress, which can cause trench mouth and gum problems.

> Daily rinsing with a new prescription mouthwash will kill the bacteria that cause gum disease. The active ingredient in the mouthwash is chlorhexidine gluconate. The mouthwash is approved by the Food and Drug Administration (FDA) and the American Dental Association (ADA). It is sold by prescription only under the brand name Peridex®. It is thought to be a breakthrough in preventing gum disease for people who cannot floss (due to physical handicaps), and people poor saliva production.

> Vitamin C may help prevent gum disease, according to

research by Dr. Robert Jacobs at the Western Human Nutrition Research Center and separate research at the University of California in San Diego (Journal of Periodontology 8/86).

• Some problems or habits increase the severity of gum disease. Most of these problems alone will not cause gum disease, according to the FDA Consumer (18:7). However, since many conditions can worsen gum disease, proper dental hygiene is especially important if you:

> Smoke or chew tobacco.
> Grind or clench your teeth (often as a reaction to stress).
> Have teeth that are not aligned properly.
> Receive poor nutrition.
> Have diabetes.
> Wear dentures that do not fit correctly.
> Are pregnant.
> Bite your nails, chew popcorn kernels, or chew ice cubes.
> Take oral contraceptives, anti-cancer drugs, steroids, anti-epilepsy drugs or durgs that cause dry mouth.

• If you are highly susceptible to gum disease, Emory University's Dwight Weathers, D.D.S. recommends eating foods that are high in vitamin A. He says that vitamin A can help strengthen gum tissue and that a deficiency of vitamin A can lead to gum problems. However, Dr. Weathers warns that vitamin A is toxic in high doses. Do not take vitamin A supplements but increase your intake of foods rich in vitamin A. Natural sources of vitamin A or carotene (which a healthy body converts into vitamin A) include eggs, whole milk products, broccoli, spinach and other green, leafy vegetables, sweet potatoes, carrots, pumpkins, and squash.

• Trench mouth, a gum disease that also causes bad breath and a metallic taste, can be treated or prevented. Dr. Weathers thinks that many people who are under a great deal of stress and who do not eat properly suffer from trench mouth. After medical treatment has cleared up the infection, good oral hygiene, a good diet featuring fresh vegetables and fruits, and learning to manage stress will help keep this gum disease from recurring.

Hair Loss and Graying
• In 1980, Dr. Abram Hoffer, a medical doctor who

advocates taking large doses of vitamins in the treatment of certain disorders, claimed that vitamin E supplementation returned his gray hair to its normal color. Another researcher has reported that very high doses of para-aminobenzoic acid (PABA) darkened his gray hair. Other researchers claim that zinc, pantothenic acid (vitamin B5), and folic acid may prevent graying of the hair or help restore color to gray hair. However, the overall effectiveness of vitamin supplements for preventing gray hair or restoring color to hair that is already gray is unknown and unproven. Taking vitamins at the Recommended Daily Dietary Allowance (RDA) is acceptable, but large doses of vitamins should be taken cautiously and with a doctor's consent because of the possibilities of serious side effects.

• Most hair loss is caused by an hereditary gene which is expressed fully in men but only slightly in women after menopuase because of a drop in protective female hormones. In women, the baldness gene usually is expressed as a slight thinning of the hair as we get older. Although both men and women lose hair, full hereditary baldness usually occurs only in men who have a double dose of the gene from both parents.

• Some problems cause permanent hair loss, Dr. Arndt explained in the Harvard Medical School Health Letter. Cancer, a severe deficiency of iron, thyroid disease, and diabetes all may cause irreversible hair loss.

• Uncommon loss of hair may be caused by a deficiency of riboflavin (vitamin B2), biotin, copper or by overdoses of vitamin A or selenium.

• Taking inositol, biotin or zinc supplements or using ointments or shampoos containing these substances is sometimes advocated for reducing hair loss or restoring hair that is already lost. The effectiveness of such treatments is usually disappointing.

• Shampooing and scrubbing daily may help prevent baldness by washing away male sex hormones in the oil in the scalp.

• Estrogen creams have been used successfully to reduce hair loss in men, but they may cause breast enlargement or other unwanted side effects.

• According to Dr. Kenneth A. Arndt, Associate Professor of Dermatology at Beth Israel Hospital, some prescription drugs

111

as well as the following traumatic events can cause a change in the body's production of hair:

> childbirth
> major surgery
> a high fever
> a lengthy or severe illness
> great emotional stress
> a strict weight-loss diet
> a large loss of blood

However, within several months the hair production should resume.

• To make the most of the hair you have, Janis Buller of Vidal Sassoon in Beverly Hills, suggests:

> Layering the hair. Hair cut in short layers will appear to be fuller.

> Use conditioners on your hair to help keep it looking full.

> Keep hair fashionably short.

> Wearing a beard will give the impression of having more hair on the head.

> Men with bald spots should not keep some hair long and try to lay it over the bald spot. It will call attention to the lack of hair, and it looks worse than the bald spot.

> Rinses and shampoos containing protein may help rebuild hair that has been physically damaged.

• To avoid unnecessary damage to your hair, limit:

> Exposure to ultraviolet rays (from sun or tanning booths).

> Exposure to heat (curling irons, hot curlers, blow dryers).

> Combing, brushing, shampooing, teasing, perming, coloring, tinting, using hair sprays, mousses, and gels.

Headaches

Headaches can have many causes but some people find that they experience more headaches as they age. Mild headaches that are not symptoms of a serious disease are usually treated with aspirin, acetaminophen or ibuprofen. Long lasting, frequent or severe headaches may be symptoms of a serious disease, so they're a signal to see your doctor. If headaches are not a symptom of another serious disease, they can be treated naturally in a number of different ways depending on what kind of headaches they are.

• The most promising new natural treatment for migraines is to take magnesium supplements. Magnesium is usually deficient in the American diet. Magnesium supplements like magnesium chloride or dolomite, which is composed of calcium carbonate and magnesium carbonate, are quite helpful to many migraine sufferers.

• Headaches can be caused by pressure to the neck or head. Wearing swimming goggles, tight fitting glasses, ties, or collars can bring on headaches in many people.

• People who suffer from migraine headaches should try these simple suggestions from the Emergency Medicine journal (16-14: 69):

> reduce the amount of caffeine you consume daily

> avoid foods that contain TYRAMINE like chicken livers or old cheese

> avoid or limit sodium glutamate, a preservative in processed foods, and sodium nitrate, which is found in cured meats like ham and hot dogs

> eat regular meals at the same time each day to avoid inadvisable blood sugar levels

> avoid or limit carbohydrates

> avoid ESTROGEN treatment

Other common causes of headaches include: sudden withdrawal from caffeine, fluorescent, bright or flickering lights, and odors from perfume, aftershave, cologne, soap or detergent. Eating ice cream or frozen treats can cause headaches after the cold dessert hits the roof of the mouth. An overdose of salt, like eating a bowl of salted nuts or potato chips, bright sunlight, and alcohol (especially red wine) can also be culprits.

Hearing Loss

• According to the National Institute on Aging, about 30% of adults between 65 and 74 and about 50% of people between 75 and 79 years suffer some degree of hearing loss. Most people are too proud to admit they have a hearing problem — and so they continue living in a hard-to-understand world.

• Hearing loss can be caused by many conditions, including changes associated with aging, heart conditions, viral infections, bacterial infections, stroke, long exposure to loud noises, tumors, some drugs, excessive ear wax, head injuries, or physical changes within the middle or inner ears.

• Hearing loss in older adults is often the result of nerve damage. Zinc supplements have been shown, in many cases, to reverse a certain type of progressive inner ear nerve loss. In a recent study, 50 hearing loss patients with a confirmed zinc deficiency were given doses of zinc at 10 times the Recommended Daily Dietary Allowance (RDA). All of the patients experienced improvement in their hearing. Large doses of zinc like those used in this study should only be given upon a physician's advice because of the possibility of serious side effects.

• If hearing loss is caused by bacterial infection, treatment with antibiotics may clear up the infection and help restore hearing.

• Many people with progressive hearing loss can be helped by eliminating substances from the diet which cause allergic deafness. If deafness is caused by a food allergy, improvement can be dramatic and total. Doctors start treatment by first giving an anti-allergy drug to the patient. If allergic reactions are causing the problem, the patient may regain his hearing within an hour after receiving the anti-allergy drug. Once the offending food substance is identified and avoided, the restoration of hearing may be permanent.

• People with hearing loss caused by a deterioration of the bone in the inner ear, called otospongeosis, have been helped by fluoride supplements. Fluoride supplements of up to 10 times the recommended daily allowance have restored hearing to some extent over a period of time in these patients. Caution: large doses of fluoride can be extremely poisonous, and any fluoride supplementation beyond the Recommended Daily Dietary Allowance (RDA) can have serious side effects and should only be undertaken with close monitoring by a physician.

• Adequate beta-carotene, vitamin A and zinc may be important for your hearing. Low blood levels of beta-carotene, vitamin A and zinc have been linked to hearing loss in studies by Erwin Lohle of the University of Freiburg in Germany.

• Researchers at University of Michigan claim vitamin D deficiency causes hearing loss because small blood vessels in the ears cannot be used. They say that vitamin D supplements help hearing loss and may even prevent deafness.

• A low-cholesterol diet that is good for your heart and arteries may also prevent hearing loss, according to a study in Finland recently published in The Laryngoscope. The researchers discovered that cholesterol restricts the amount of blood that flows through the small arteries in the ear, and hearing loss develops. In a study of 4,000 people, hearing improved on a low-fat diet but worsened when fatty foods were given. See our section on **Cholesterol Reduction** for information on how to lower your cholesterol intake.

• Magnesium deficiency has also been linked to poor hearing, according to research in the Journal of the Acoustical Society of America. Loud noises actually lower the amount of magnesium in the ear. This causes the blood vessels there to constrict which leads to increased hearing loss.

• Ringing in the ears, known as tinnitus, may be helped by proper nutrition, says Paul Yanick, executive director of the Hearing and Tinnitus Help Association. Yanick believes that proper nutrition creates a chemical balance which helps to stabilize ear sounds.

One of the first signs of aspirin overdose is tinnitus. This can occur after one large dose or after taking small doses over a period of time. The tinnitus is not permanent. It disappears after the aspirin is discontinued, and there is no permanent hearing loss. However, anyone who experiences ringing in the ears while he is taking aspirin should contact his doctor, since other serious problems may result from aspirin overdose. Tinnitus can also be a side effect of prescription drugs.

• Some cases of hearing loss can be corrected by doing things as simple as having a physician remove excessive ear wax, avoiding loud noises from machinery or loudspeakers, or trying an alternate prescription drug if hearing loss is a side effect of medication.

Heart Problems

• Heart attacks are unknown or extremely rare among primitive people. They also were rare in the U.S. up until 70 years ago when the rate began to skyrocket. If you have one of these health problems or habits, you are at a high risk of developing heart problems, including a heart attack:

> smoking or breathing cigarette smoke
> high blood pressure
> family history of heart disease or heart attacks
> eating foods that are high in fat or cholesterol
> eating large amounts of sugar and other low-fiber foods
> drinking large quantities of coffee
> alcoholism
> being overweight
> having gout or diabetes
> being inactive
> taking birth control pills
> taking over-the-counter diet pills containing phenyl-propanolamine (PPA) or crash dieting
> drinking soft water
> drinking heavily chlorinated water
> a high white-blood cell count
> a stressful lifestyle

Most of the risk factors for heart problems, except for one's personal family history, can be avoided. The lifestyle you have chosen and the foods you eat can affect your risk of heart problems.

• Lower high blood pressure. Reducing high blood pressure (hypertension) helps lessen the chance of developing heart problems and artery disease. See our section on **Blood Pressure — High** for helpful information on how to control high blood pressure.

• Be aware of heredity. People who come from families where their parents or other close relatives have had heart disease are at greater risk than people who come from families with low rates of heart problems. Although heredity is not controllable, the presence of heart problems in a close family member is a high risk factor and a warning sign that all possible precautions should be taken.

• Quit smoking to reduce chances of heart disease. Heavy

cigarette smokers have twice the death rate from coronary heart disease as non-smokers. Non-smokers who live in the same house with a heavy cigarette smoker have higher death rates than those who don't live with smokers. Heavy cigarette smokers have a life expectancy as much as ten years less than that of non-smokers.

Switching from cigarettes to cigars does not help reduce your risk of having a heart attack, reports the British Medical Journal (6/15/87). Smoking five cigars a day still increases your risk of heart attack by 4.5 times the risk of a nonsmoker, according to the research.

Smoking seems to increase the risk of a heart attack, even if you don't have hardening of the arteries, according to new research from Emory University in Atlanta. In a group of people under 60 years old who did not have hardening of the arteries but suffered heart attacks, over 71% had a history of smoking. Only 48 people were involved in the study, so further studies will be needed to conclusively prove the findings.

• Reduce the amount of fat in your diet, especially saturated fats, which are usually found in meat and dairy products. Fat should be reduced to 30% of total calorie intake, which is the level recommended by the American Heart Association. Other health groups have recommended reducing dietary fat to levels as low as 10-15%. These levels are substantially lower than the levels found in typical American diets.

• Lower your blood cholesterol. It's a good practice to measure cholesterol and its HDL (high-density lipoprotein) and LDL (low-density lipoprotein) fractions every time blood is drawn for a physical exam. High LDL levels are harmful, but high HDL levels can help prevent heart problems.

See our section on **Cholesterol Build Up** for specific information on how you can reduce your fat and cholesterol intake.

When niacin (vitamin B3) is taken in high doses it has been shown to reduce the amount of cholesterol in the blood (Journal of the American Medical Association JAMA:79). In a study of heart attack victims, it was found that people who took high doses of niacin had an 11% lower death rate than those who did not. Niacin must be administered in high doses to be effective against heart disease and cholesterol. Because of the significant side effects of high doses of niacin, such as irregular heartbeat, it should be taken only under a doctor's supervision. Some people, such as those with high blood pressure, diabetes, gout or ulcers, should not take niacin at all. The niacinamide form of the vitamin should not be used because it does not lower blood fats by a significant amount. Food sources for niacin include yeast, fish, poultry, liver, meat, whole-grain products (except corn which contains an inactive form of niacin), peanuts, potatoes, beans and mushrooms.

• Heavy coffee drinkers increase their risk of heart disease by as much as three times the risk of non-coffee drinkers, according to a study at Johns Hopkins Medical Institute in Baltimore. The researchers found that men who drank five or more cups of coffee daily were 2.8 times as likely to develop coronary artery (or heart) disease. The study, published in the New England Journal of Medicine (315:16,977-82), included 1,130 males. It seems that an occasional cup of coffee is acceptable, but heavy coffee drinking should be avoided. The more coffee you drink, the more you are increasing your risk of coronary artery disease, angina and a sudden heart attack, the researchers concluded.

If you already have heart problems, avoid coffee, or limit yourself to two cups a day. Coffee can overstimulate the heart and decrease the effectiveness of certain angina and blood-pressure medications, according to Cardiac Alert (8:5). The caffeine in coffee causes an increase in the heart rate which can be very dangerous to someone with heart problems. Cardiac Alert recommends that all coffee, with or without caffeine, should be avoided by people with heart or artery problems.

• Avoid alcohol if it is a heavy habit. Alcoholism or heavy consumption of alcoholic beverages is a definite risk factor which leads to an increased rate of heart attacks. Small amounts of alcohol (the equivalent of one or two small beers a day) is not harmful to the heart.

• People who are overweight need to gradually lose weight until normal weight levels are reached and maintained. The heavier an obese person is, the more likely he is to have a heart attack. Excess pounds put extra strain on the heart.

• Up to 60% of Americans are at risk of developing coronary heart disease because they are physically inactive, according to the <u>Morbidity</u> <u>and</u> <u>Mortality</u> <u>Weekly</u> <u>Report</u> by the Centers for Disease Control. Although researchers are not sure exactly how much exercise is needed, they believe that inactivity is a risk as great as high levels of cholesterol, high blood pressure or smoking.

A recent study at the University of Pittsburgh found that the main link between exercise and prevention of heart disease was the regularity of exercise. They discovered that mailmen who walked an average of five miles a day had higher blood levels of HDL's (the good, protective type of cholesterol). Since the walks were continuously interrupted, the exercise could not be classed as aerobic. The researchers felt that the key was exercising every day rather than being inactive.

Beware of sudden spurts of strenuous activity. Moderate, medically-supervised, regular exercise, started gradually, may help in living with or recovering from certain heart problems. However, sudden spurts of activity, like exercising vigorously only on weekends or just because you "feel like" exercising, is NOT good for your heart and arteries, says Dr. Peter J. Steincrohn. It is a paradox that many studies show that regular, sustained aerobic exercise strengthens the heart and helps circulation while other studies show that sudden, unaccustomed bursts of exercise can lead to heart attacks in susceptible people.

Shoveling snow requires a sudden spurt of very strenuous upper-body activity, so it should be avoided by people with heart problems. Using a snow blower or hiring someone else to shovel is best.

• Before you shower after exercising, cool down, advises Dr. John Cantwell in the <u>American</u> <u>Medical</u> <u>Journal</u> (252:429). Cantwell, the team doctor for the Atlanta Braves baseball club, says that showering too soon after exercising can cause spasms in your arteries or a sharp decrease in blood pressure. Exercise causes a fall in blood pressure because blood tends to collect in the legs after completing the exercise, he explains. If you take a hot or warm shower while in this condition, the hot water can dilate (enlarge) the blood vessels and create an even greater drop in blood pressure. On the other hand, a cold shower can raise the blood pressure, and place a sudden strain on the heart. This could cause some arteries to spasm, explains the doctor. To avoid any bad effects, Dr. Cantwell says that you should completely cool down after exercising and before heading for the showers.

• A high white blood cell count increases a person's risk of having heart disease. According to a recent study at the University of Minnesota, people with a high white blood cell (WBC) count have an increased risk of developing heart disease. The abnormally high level of white blood cells can cause damage to the artery walls, says Dr. Richard Grimm, Jr. Smoking, another risk factor in heart disease, is extremely dangerous when combined with a high white blood cell count, Dr. Grimm warns.

• Some vitamins and minerals are claimed to help fight heart problems:

> Inositol and vitamin E supplements may help protect the heart.

> A deficiency of copper causes damage to the heart and arteries.

> Heart patients who have a high intake of processed carbohydrates such as sugar and white flour have been found to have lower levels of thiamine (vitamin B1) in the body. Thiamine is needed for muscle tone and in order for energy to be supplied to the heart muscle.

> Potassium supplements are claimed to lower the rate of heart disease and heart attacks.

> Zinc has been reported to reduce the rate of heart disease.

> Studies by Kurt A. Oster, M.D. and others indicate that large doses of folic acid (as much as 80 mg. per day) may be helpful in the treatment and prevention of heart disease. Larger, controlled studies are necessary to confirm this. Don't try taking such large doses without your doctor's approval because of possibly dangerous side effects.

> Low sodium diets seem to reduce the chances of suffering from heart and blood vessel disorders.

> Chromium supplements may aid in the treatment of maturity-onset diabetes and the heart and circulation problems associated with diabetes.

> Extreme vitamin D overdose can lead to heart failure. An overdose of vitamin A can lead to poor heart rhythm from high levels of blood calcium associated with vitamin A poisoning.

> A deficiency of vitamin B12 or biotin can lead to heart

pain. An iodine deficiency can lead to heart palpitations.

> People living in areas in the United States and other countries with low levels of naturally occuring selenium have much higher rates of heart disease.

> Regular supplements of the "heart protecting" vitamins C and E and the mineral selenium may not prevent a heart attack, but they may help to keep the heart living through the trauma of a heart attack, according to Joe McCord at the University of South Alabama College of Medicine. Since the worst damage to the heart often occurs immediately after the heart attack, McCord claims that if the body has an adequate supply of vitamins C and E and selenium, the heart muscle will have a better chance of survival.

• Veins in your neck that suddenly begin to stand out could be a warning sign of heart problems. According to Dr. Frank Field in Family Circle magazine (10/1/86), the veins in your neck can fill with blood when a heart is failing. Many heart specialists examine the neck as part of their routine check-ups. If you notice a change in the veins of your neck, contact your doctor.

• Avoid holding your breath when straining, says Cardiac Alert newsletter. This "Valsalva Maneuver" counteracts the natural breathing pattern when you are trying to lift, pull, push or move something. Many times, people hold their breath and groan while straining. The Valsalva Maneuver is especially common during weight-lifting. Holding your breath during these strenuous times causes your blood pressure to skyrocket and puts additional pressure on your heart and arteries.

Practice breathing in and out slowly and steadily. Consciously breathe during any strenuous activity. Then, when lifting or moving something, be sure to have enough people or support to properly help you move the object.

Avoid all straining during bowel movements. As well as increasing your blood pressure, the strain may cause hemorrhoids and bowel problems. High fiber diets help people avoid straining at stool.

• Be very careful in the mornings. A recent study by Harvard University researchers showed that most sudden cardiac deaths occur between 6:00 a.m. and noon. After reviewing over 2,000 death certificates of heart attack victims, the researchers published their findings in the journal Circulation. Doctors are not exactly sure what factors increase the risk of an early morning death. Perhaps the normal rise in blood pressure that is experienced in the morning or the increased production of blood platelets which cause blood to clot contribute to causing heart attacks in the morning. Previous victims of heart attacks and people with heart problems should take extra care to avoid exertion before noon.

• If you live in a climate with a severe winter, avoid unnecessary stress on your heart and circulation system. Dress properly and don't overexpose yourself to cold weather. Avoid physical exertion, especially shoveling snow, in the cold outdoors. Exertion, especially in cold weather, often causes heart attacks.

• Many people at high risk for heart problems do as well taking medicine as they do with major surgery, reveals a study by Dr. Robert Luchi at the Veterans Administration Medical Center in Houston. Two groups of people with unstable angina, which is considered to be a high risk factor for heart disease, were treated with either heart bypass surgery or with medicine. Dr. Luchi found that both groups had a similar rate of heart attacks. Since drug treatment is less traumatic and less expensive than surgery, the report suggests that drug therapy should be the treatment of choice. However, the researchers warned that the hearts of the people who took medicine were less efficient pumps than those of the people who had undergone heart surgery. (The New England Journal of Medicine 316: 16, 977-84).

• Regular examinations by the physician are extremely important for patients taking digoxin because it is very easy to get too much or too little digoxin in the bloodstream. Either of these conditions is dangerous. Studies have shown that of those people who have died while on digoxin therapy, 20% had toxic blood levels of digoxin. People receiving digitalis or other heart medication should not take calcium ascorbate (a vitamin C formulation), since irregular heartbeats may occur.

• For some heart patients, an aspirin a day can reduce the chance of having another heart attack, the Food and Drug Administration (FDA) says. One aspirin tablet per day can cut heart attacks by 20% for some people who have already had heart attacks, to as much as 50% in men who have unstable angina. Aspirin is not a substitute for other preventative therapies for heart attacks, cautioned FDA commissioner Frank E. Young, M.D. He advises that patients consult their physicians before starting daily aspirin as therapy. The studies do not show whether aspirin would be effective in preventing heart attacks in healthy people, or just in people with history of heart attacks or angina.

• Avoid areas of air pollution. Ozone, sulfur dioxide, nitrogen dioxide, cigarette smoke, carbon monoxide, hydrocarbons, nitrogen oxide and photochemical substances are air pollutants that can aggravate heart problems.

• Your working conditions may be increasing the severity of your heart problems, Dr. Jorge C. Rios warns in Cardiac Alert (8:5). Breathing polluted air in your workplace, working in extremely hot temperatures, working under stress, and working with high noise levels can contribute to heart problems and angina, says Dr. Rios.

• Living at high altitudes may not be as harmful to the heart as has been thought. In the past, doctors thought that high altitudes caused heart problems; however, new research by the American Heart Association shows that the opposite may be true. James K. Alexander, M.D. of Baylor College of Medicine in Houston participated in the study called Operation Everest Two. Over a 40-day span, seven men were put into a low-pressure chamber that simulated the effects of 29,000 feet altitude. Dr. Alexander said they were surprised to discover that the heart actually seemed to do better at high altitude! However, sudden changes to high altitudes should be avoided, and people with severe heart disease may be helped by moving to low altitudes. Ask your physician for advice.

• A "strong belief in a supreme being" may lower your risk of heart disease, according to a study published in the International Journal of Cardiology (1/86). The study of over 500 men and women found that devout Jews had lower heart-attack rates than non-practicing Jews. In the researchers' own words, "the strong belief in a supreme being and the role of prayer may in themselves be protective."

• Men with heart disease have high blood levels of Immunoglobulin E (IgE), a substance related to allergies, reports

Dr. Michael Criqui in the <u>American</u> <u>Journal</u> <u>of</u> <u>Medicine</u> (6/1/87). The blood levels of IgE were up to 119% higher in men who had heart disease than in men without heart problems. There was no difference in the IgE levels in women with or without heart disease. Whether men with allergies are at higher risk of developing heart disease is not known. The study did not show how heart disease and high IgE levels are related, but Dr. Criqui is planning to do further research on the subject.

• Some scientific studies have indicated that creased earlobes are associated with the development of heart disease. However, a recent study in the <u>Archives</u> <u>of</u> <u>Internal</u> <u>Medicine</u> (147:65-66) reports that the incidence of creased earlobes and the incidence of heart disease both increase with age. The study questioned the relationship between the two conditions. If you have or develop creased earlobes, do not feel that it necessarily means that you have heart disease.

• Women who have their ovaries removed should have estrogen-replacement therapy to lower their risk of heart disease, reports <u>The</u> <u>New</u> <u>England</u> <u>Journal</u> <u>of</u> <u>Medicine</u> (316: 1105-10). Women who had their ovaries removed and did NOT take estrogen had twice the risk of developing heart disease, according to the study conducted at Harvard Medical School.

• A new blood test could help identify people at high risk for developing heart disease, reports <u>American</u> <u>Health</u> (6:4). The blood test is under consideration for approval by the Food and Drug Administration (FDA). The test is manufactured and developed by California Biotechnology. It can identify certain factors that are known to affect heart disease including:

> cholesterol receptors that control the levels of low and high lipoprotein levels (LDL's and HDL's)

> molecules, called apolipoproteins, that carry blood cholesterol

> certain hormones related to blood pressure

> insulin production levels

• Recovering from a heart attack can be difficult, especially when a spouse is worried about your every move. Researchers at Stanford University tried an experiment that allowed the spouse to participate in the physical therapy of the heart attack victim. Not only did they watch the activities, they had to perform the same treadmill stress tests, side-by-side with their spouses. According to an article in <u>Body</u> <u>Bulletin</u>, the loving spouse could see and experience the physical activity and stress of the treadmill. Once they knew how their mates had endured the exercise, they didn't worry about them as much at home during the recovery. The spouses encouraged their partners and were tolerant of their activities. With the spouses' support, recovery was less stressful and a little easier for the heart attack victim.

• Lifestyles and stress can affect each person's chances for survival following a heart attack. According to research published in <u>The</u> <u>New</u> <u>England</u> <u>Journal</u> <u>of</u> <u>Medicine</u> (311: 552), loneliness and high levels of stress decrease chances for survival in a person recovering from a heart attack. People who were not able to communicate effectively with their doctors and other medical staff, or who were not able to discuss problems with family or close friends, or who didn't participate in many social events had a lower survival rate than people who had a supportive and close family. Patients who participated in social and church activities and felt they could talk to their doctors about their problems experienced quicker recoveries.

Stress factors such as not being satisfied with work, serious family problems or violent events also decrease a patient's chances for survival after a heart attack. Therefore, to increase your chances for survival after a heart attack: avoid stressful situations, remain or become socially active, and draw close to your family, friends and church.

• Pets may be helpful in increasing your chances of survival after a heart attack. According to one study of 92 patients, 11 of the 29 people without pets died within a year of their hospitalization. However, only 3 of the 59 people who had pets died within the same amount of time. Since the study included several variables like exercise, proper nutrition and diet, the research does not prove that pets alone improve survival rates. However, many doctors and therapists feel that pets provide love, support, an opportunity for exercise and a reason for living. Even though heart-attack patients generally have to rely on others for care, by having a pet they are reassured of their own worth since another creature depends on them. Pets also help people fight loneliness and depression, which can be devastating after a heart-attack.

Pets aren't for everyone. Before urging a heart attack survivor to own a pet, be sure that he is willing and able to take care of it.

• Portable defibrillators, like the machines used in hospital emergency rooms to "shock" the heart into restarting, could save thousands of lives. The defibrillator delivers a specified amount of electric current to a heart with an irregular heartbeat.

Thousands of Americans suffer from heart attacks every year and are considered at high risk for having another heart attack. Dr. Richard O. Cummins, a researcher at the University of Washington, explains that the defibrillators could be used by family members, office workers, airline attendants, and rural emergency services. Dr. Cummins explained that CPR (cardiopulmonary resuscitation) helps keep a person alive until the heart can be restarted, but many times the person dies before they can receive medical assistance. Spouses and co-workers of people at high risk for heart attacks can receive just four hours of training and be able to use a portable defibrillator. Portable defibrillators are now approved and available in the U.S. but must be prescribed by a doctor.

Heartburn — see: Indigestion

Heart Pain — see: Angina Pectoris

Heat Stroke

• Heat stroke is a result of the body's inability to regulate its temperature. Heat exhaustion is less serious. It's caused by an excessive loss of body fluids, according to The Merck Manual.

If heat stroke is suspected (hard rapid pulse, very high body temperature, hot dry skin), the person should be immersed in cold water or ice and emergency medical services should be contacted immediately. However, do not allow the person's temperature to drop below normal.

If heat exhaustion is suspected (pale clammy skin, weak slow pulse faintness and low blood pressure) the lost fluids need to be replaced, and the person should rest flat or with his head between his knees. He should drink lots of water or mineral replacement beverages like Gatorade®, eat some highly salted food (like nuts or potato chips) and contact the doctor.

• The U.S. Government reports that certain people are at a high risk of suffering from overheating, including those who:
> are over 65 years of age
> have diabetes
> have cystic fibrosis
> are overweight
> have heart problems
> have had a stroke
> have circulation problems
> are taking diuretic drugs
> are taking drugs for Parkinson's disease

• Heat exhaustion and heat stroke can be prevented by proper care and planning. Take the following precautions during hot weather, particularly if you are in any of the high-risk categories:

> Wear loose, comfortable clothing that covers your shoulders. Lightweight, light-colored clothing is best. Make sure that everything is loose, including your underwear. Loose clothing will help the air circulate and keep you cooler.

> Wear a hat when in the sun or carry an umbrella. However, remember to take the hat off when you are in the shade so that heat will be able to escape through your head. If you leave your hat on, you may risk heat build-up.

> Stay in air-conditioned places during the heat of the day. If you cannot afford an air-conditioner, visit a library, shopping mall, community center, movie theater, church, museum or other place that is air-conditioned.

> Use fans to help circulate air during the day and to draw in cooler air in the evenings.

> Avoid extended outdoor activities, especially in the heat of the day. Plan outdoor events for the early morning or evening. Avoid long periods of outdoor water sports. Although the water will help you feel comfortable, you may be receiving too much exposure to the sun and could still suffer from heat exhaustion.

> Rest or do "quiet" activities as much as possible. Exercise

or physical activity in hot weather will put additional strain on your heart.

> Drink at least eight glasses of water a day. Water is better than any other drink to help your body maintain a healthy temperature. Do not drink alcohol because it causes a quick loss of body liquids. If you have a medical problem that is affected by drinking a large quantity of fluids, ask your doctor how much liquid you should be drinking every day.

> Do not eat hot foods or heavy meals. Eat plenty of fresh fruit and vegetables. As well as providing good nutrition and fiber, fresh fruit will add to the water your body receives.

> Consider soaking in a tub of cool water every evening. Avoid hot baths or showers because they increase your body temperature.

> Avoid sunbathing. As well as unnecessarily raising your body temperature, exposure to the sun is known to cause skin cancer.

> Your body needs time to adjust to extreme temperatures. If summer comes quickly and the temperature is unseasonally hot, you need to be more careful than you do later in the summer. If you travel to a tropical climate from a cooler climate, allow time for your body to adjust.

• Certain drugs, combined with high humidity and warm temperatures, may lead to heatstroke. Anticholinergics (certain asthma medications) and antipsychotic drugs (phenothiazines) affect the central nervous system and distort the body's natural thermostat.

Extra care to avoid overheating during exercise should be taken by people who use drugs which can cause decreased sweating. Some of these drugs include: Belladenal®, Bellergal®, Chardonna-2®, Comhist®, Dicyclomine®, Donnatal®, Donnazyme®, Kinesed®, Librax®, Wigran-PS®, antidyskinetics, anti-depressants and drugs to treat Parkinson's disease.

Hemorrhoids
• Hemorrhoids are enlarged, dilated veins of the rectal and anal passages. They can occur at any age, but they are found

more often as people get older.

• Most hemorrhoids are caused by eating a diet low in dietary fiber, which is the fiber found in bran, whole grain products, and in many vegetables such as corn and beans. Because of the lack of fiber, the stool matter is dry and hard, and bowel movements put a great strain on the rectal area. Not only are hemorrhoids caused by lack of dietary fiber, but in almost all cases their symptoms can be relieved by putting fiber back into the regular diet.

This little known health secret is simple and effective in treating hemorrhoids. Start the day with a good whole grain cereal for breakfast, eat a sandwich on some whole-grain bread for lunch and eat lots of fresh vegetables and whole-grain rolls for supper. Almost everyone who adds this natural fiber to his diet ceases to be bothered by hemorrhoid symptoms within a short period of time.

Unfortunately, the weakness in the veins which causes hemorrhoids will remain even when fiber is added back into the diet. If a person who has had hemorrhoid problems returns to a low fiber diet, the hemorrhoids will flare up again.

• Drinking at least eight glasses of water each day also helps to keep the stool soft. Dietary fiber soaks up water in the digestive tract and becomes soft and easy to pass.

• Because of the extra pressure within the abdomen, hemorrhoids often afflict pregnant women as well as people with jobs that require many hours of sitting. These people should be particularly careful to eat a high-fiber diet, to get plenty of exercise, (including walking for at least 10 minutes every two hours), and to exercise the rectal muscles by squeezing and releasing them several times daily.

• If you suffer from hemorrhoids, you may need to try these methods to relieve the pain:

> Soak in a tub of hot water, (or 1/4 cup witch hazel in a basin of warm water) three or four times a day.

> Lie on your side or your stomach rather than sitting.

> Keep your rectal area very clean.

> Try applying a bag of ice to relieve swelling in the inflamed area.

> Use moistened toilet paper to avoid aggravating the area.

> Do not scratch hemorrhoids because scratching will only cause further irritation.

> Check with your doctor for special instructions on medication. Over the counter products containing yeast extract, like Preparation H®, are very effective according to recent scientific studies.

• Developing good toilet habits is also important to prevent hemorrhoids from occurring. Always go to the restroom when you need to. If you put off going, your body will eventually lose its natural mechanism which tells you when to have a bowel movement. Never sit and strain to have a bowel movement — if you are eating properly, bowel movements should be quick and natural. You should usually be able to have a bowel movement easily. Just relax and let your body work naturally.

• Never use artificial laxatives or enemas regularly. Natural laxatives like prunes, raisins, other dried fruit, vegetables, whole grain products and bran should be part of your regular diet. If your diet is deficient in those foods, supplements containing psyllium mucilloid are an alternative source of bulk. Artificial laxatives destroy the body's own ability to eliminate waste properly. If you start taking them, you will be caught in a vicious circle where you have to rely on them in order to have a bowel movement.

Hiatus Hernia

• Hiatus (or hiatal) hernia occurs when the sphincter muscle between the esophagus and the stomach becomes separated from the surrounding tissues. The muscle is intended to keep food and acid from the stomach from being regurgitated up into the esophagus. When the sphincter muscle cannot do its job effectively, because of hiatus hernia or poor muscle tone, acids irritate the esophagus and throat. Pain, commonly called heartburn, is often experienced. Women over 40 are at the highest risk of developing a hiatus hernia. Severe hiatus hernia may have to be repaired by surgery, but natural methods of treatment often can make heartburn go away.

• Heartburn can be caused by using tobacco. Nicotine evidently causes the sphincter muscle to lose tone. Quit using

cigarettes, pipes, cigars, chewing tobacco, or snuff.
- Heartburn during the night can be caused by eating too close to the time you lie down to sleep. Don't eat large meals or eat within three hours of bedtime. Avoid overeating at any time of the day.
- If you are regularly bothered by indigestion or heartburn at night, try raising the head of your bed by six to ten inches. Use wooden blocks or bricks under the legs at the head of bed. This should create enough difference in the level of your head and your stomach so that acid will not flow up out of the stomach.
- During the day, do not lie down if you are bothered by heartburn. Sitting or standing helps to keep the stomach acids in the stomach.
- Hiatus hernia can be caused by or aggravated by obesity. Losing weight, especially if you are fat around the stomach, may help. Consult your doctor for diet and exercise suggestions.
- Avoid bending over. Bending puts pressure on your abdomen, which can aggravate heartburn.
- Do not wear tight clothes, girdles, or belts.
- Chocolate, peppermint, tobacco of any kind, aspirin, coffee, tea, alcohol, fried foods, tomato products, onion, garlic, citrus fruits and juices, spicy or fatty foods can all cause problems and should be avoided.
- Constipation can cause problems. Increasing the amount of fiber in the diet may eliminate constipation and reduce the additional pressure on the stomach. Also see our report on **Constipation** in this book.
- During pregnancy, the additional pressure on the abdominal muscles can cause heartburn. The discomfort it brings can temporarily be treated with antacids. The types of antacids which coat the stomach and which are dispensed in liquid form are most effective in relieving heartburn.
- Develop good eating habits. Eat slowly. This will reduce the amount of air you swallow. Swallowed air aggravates heartburn.
- To further reduce the amount of air you swallow, don't talk while you are eating, don't drink carbonated soft drinks and don't chew gum.
- Eat smaller meals. If you can eat six small meals rather

than three large meals, you should experience less heartburn.

High Blood Pressure — see: Blood
   Pressure — High.

Hip Fractures
•   Hip fractures often occur in older people because the bones lose density and strength in many people as they get older. When an older person breaks a hip, death often follows because of complications of being bedridden while recovering from the broken hip. Older people who are bedridden often get blood clots, which may travel to the lungs or to the brain and cause serious injury or strokes.

•   Older people should make sure that hazardous areas are made safe. Put non-skid strips on the bottom of the bathtub or shower and install a handrail as well. Remove or tape down loose throw rugs in the house, especially from hallways where a person may slip while making a turn. Handrails should be put up beside all stairs and steps.

•   There are also ways to strengthen bones so that a fall might not cause a fracture. Addition of calcium and vitamin D to the diet, within the Recommended Daily Dietary allowance (RDA), often decreases the normal loss of bone mass in older people. The bone degeneration of osteoporosis occurs in older women especially.

>   Fluoride supplements are claimed to provide stronger bones, fewer bone fractures, and less osteoporosis in older women. This should be taken only under a doctor's supervision, because of dangerous side effects, however.

>   Large doses of choline upsets the natural balance of phosphorus and calcium in the bones. Therefore, large doses of choline may contribute to bone degeneration and increased fractures.

>   Taking more than the RDA of phosphorus may eliminate calcium from the bones. Excessive phosphorus in the diet, particularly from soft drinks, contributes to osteoporosis and bone fractures.

See also **Osteoporosis.**

Hormonal Changes — see: Menopause.

Hypertension — see: **Blood Pressure — High.**

Impotence

• Impotence usually occurs for physical reasons and not psychological reasons. It occurs more often as men get older.

• According to the journal <u>Urology</u> (April 1986), smoking is the biggest factor in causing impotence. In a study of over 1,000 men suffering from impotence, 78% were smokers. Smoking, and the narrowing of the blood vessels that it causes, was more strongly related to impotence than high blood pressure, age, or diabetes, which are all possible contributing factors.

• Doctors have recently discovered that "hardening of the arteries," which is a major factor in heart disease, heart attacks and strokes, can also lead to impotence. Studies in Paris, France, reported in the medical journal, <u>The Lancet</u>, showed that men with cardiovascular disease factors like diabetes or high blood pressure, those who smoke or those who have a high concentration of blood fats (lipids) are at an increased risk of suffering from impotence. A man's ability to achieve and maintain an erection is based on a good blood supply to the penis, so hardening of the arteries can cause impotence. Doctors recommend that men with impotence problems should follow the same lifestyle changes as those recommended for people with cardiovascular problems. Many cases of impotence are resolved by these simple changes.

> reduce the amount of cholesterol and fats from the diet
> quit smoking
> maintain a regular exercise program.

• Impotence is often a side effect of a prescription drug. According to <u>UCLA Health Insights</u>, sixteen of the top 200 prescription drugs cause impotence as a side effect. Many drugs prescribed for high blood pressure, like diuretics (nicknamed water pills) and Tagamet® (an anti-ulcer drug) can cause impotence. Any man who suddenly develops impotence while on a prescription medication should contact his physician immediately. Having your doctor change your drugs may eliminate impotence.

• Lowering blood pressure by natural means may enable a doctor to take a patient off the medicine which may be causing or contributing to impotence.

• Taking vitamin E has been advocated by some people to increase sexual function and to combat impotence. Vitamin E is proven to increase fertility in some people, but there is no evidence that it increases sexual drive or reduces impotence. As a matter of fact, one study showed that taking large doses of vitamin E may cause reduced sexual function.

• Taking zinc supplements has been reported to improve some cases of impotence, but its effectiveness is unproven. Large doses of zinc supplements can be dangerous, so any zinc supplementation should be within the Recommended Daily Dietary Allowance (RDA) of 15 mg. per day for adults.

• Abuse of alcohol or use of illegal drugs can cause impotence. Even moderate consumption of alcohol can cause temporary impotence.

• Good overall health is the best way to combat many cases of impotence. Regular, daily exercise, keeping weight under control and eating a healthy diet with lots of whole grain products and little fat can improve overall health and, in some cases, counteract a tendency towards impotence.

• A mild stimulant, like caffeine in coffee, sometimes will help reduce impotence.

• Any prolonged physical disease, especially kidney disease or a disease that affects male hormone secretion, can cause impotence in a man.

• Impotence often is a consequence of nerve damage during operations for removal of cancerous prostate glands, because much of the surrounding tissue is also removed. However, impotence rarely occurs as a result of operations to relieve constriction from an enlarged prostate gland which is non-cancerous, since this operation is less radical. Doctors at Johns Hopkins University have developed a technique of removing a cancerous prostate that avoids nerve damage in most cases and preserves sexual function. Impotence caused by nerve damage from an operation cannot be corrected, except by unusual methods such as surgical implants in the penis.

• Impotence infrequently can be caused by psychological reasons such as:
> stress
> fear of not being able to sexually perform
> fear of causing unwanted pregnancy
> worries about the relationship between the sex partners
> problems with the man's feelings about sexuality
> being afraid of sex after surgery, heart attack or other major health problem.

Professional counselling and learning how to properly deal with stress may help restore potency if the cause is psychological.

Also see: **Sex Drive**.

Indigestion

• Indigestion, if it is not caused by an infectious illness or other serious disease, is usually caused by intolerance to foods. Milk and milk products are the chief offenders. Other foods such as corn, processed meats, chocolate, peppermint, tobacco of any kind, aspirin, coffee, tea, fried foods, tomato products, onion, garlic, citrus fruits and juices, and spicy or fatty foods can all cause indigestion and should be avoided if possible. See your doctor to make sure indigestion is not caused by any serious disease; if it's not, start eliminating foods from the diet to see if you can find the causes.

• During the day, do not lie down if you are bothered by indigestion. Lying down makes the problem worse. Sitting up or standing helps the stomach acids remain in the stomach. Also, avoid bending over. This puts more pressure on your abdomen, which can aggravate indigestion.

• Indigestion or heartburn during the night can be caused by eating too close to the time you lie down to sleep. Doctors recommend that people should not eat for two to three hours before bedtime. While sleeping, all your body functions slow down. The stomach does not digest food as quickly, and too much stomach acid is produced. Because you are lying down while sleeping, some of the excess acid can "back up," causing irritation in the stomach and esophagus. If you are regularly bothered by indigestion in the night, try raising the head of your bed by six inches. This should create enough difference in the level between your head and your stomach so the acid cannot flow up out of the stomach.

• Sleeping on a water bed can aggravate indigestion, according to new research at the University of Rochester in New York State (Journal of the American Medical Association: JAMA 257:15, 2033). Sensations of floating and the pull of gravity may cause indigestion, says the report. Water beds with baffles that stop the free flow of water are recommended to reduce the moving sensations. When reclining on a water bed as on a regular bed, be sure that your head is not lower than your stomach, or stomach acid may escape and create indigestion.

• Develop good eating habits. Eat slowly by putting your knife and fork down between bites. This will slow down your eating and reduce the amount of air you swallow with each bite. Since much indigestion is caused by overeating, eating smaller meals will help reduce the problem. It takes approximately 20 minutes for your appetite center to be satisfied when eating, so by eating slowly you are also likely to eat less.

• Losing weight, especially in your waist, may be helpful in reducing the amount of indigestion you experience. Do not wear tight clothes, girdles or belts. Excess weight or tight clothing around the stomach creates pressure on the stomach that can cause indigestion. Many women experience indigestion problems during pregnancy because of the extra pressure on their stomachs.

• Indigestion may be caused by several over-the-counter or prescription drugs including: aspirin, ibuprofen (Motrin®, Advil®, Nuprin®), anti-histamines, anti-inflammatory drugs used to treat arthritis, some antibiotics, uric acid inhibitors used to treat gout, sedatives, blood vessel enlarging drugs, narcotics, antidepressants and pain relievers. If you are taking any medicine, discuss your indigestion problem with your doctor, and try to reduce or eliminate any drugs that might be causing the trouble.

To avoid indigestion when taking aspirin, ibuprofen, over-the-counter pain-relievers, or vitamin C in the form of ascorbic acid :

> Always take aspirin, ibuprofen or ascorbic acid only after

eating.

> Take them with a full glass of milk or water. Never take aspirin, ibuprofen or ascorbic acid with an acidic juice, citrus fruit or alcohol.

> If aspirin and ibuprofen continue to cause indigestion, consider switching to an enteric-coated brand, or change to acetaminophen. Enteric-coating allows the drugs to be released in the bowel instead of the stomach, which will reduce or eliminate stomach irritation. However, the enteric-coated drug will take several hours to become effective.

> Do not take aspirin and vitamin C together. This can increase the risk and severity of indigestion.

> Vitamin C in the form of ascorbic acid should always be taken with food or with a large amount of water and an antacid.

• Estrogens can weaken the sphincter muscle that keeps stomach acids in the stomach. Any woman taking estrogens, or a pregnant woman who has a natural increase in estrogen production, is more likely to suffer from indigestion, according to the Harvard Medical School Health Letter.

• Do not take antacids if you are taking prescription medication or aspirin, according to The Medical Letter Handbook of Drug Interactions. Antacids react with many types of medication, so discuss it with your pharmacist or doctor before you take antacids with:

> benzodiazepines(Valium®, Librium®, Xanax®)
> cimetidine (Tagamet®)
> corticosteroids
> digoxin
> fluoride
> indomethacin (Indocin®)
> isoniazid
> pseudoephedrine (Sudafed®)
> ranitidine (Zantac®)
> salicylates (like aspirin)
> tetracyclines
> thiazide diuretics (like Diuril® and Hygroton®)

• Avoid comfrey-pepsin capsules available for indigestion in health food stores. According to The New England Journal of Medicine (315:17,1095) comfrey roots contain a substance known as pyrolizidine which can lead to liver problems and cancer. The journal warns that taking comfrey-pepsin capsules over a period of several months could be very dangerous.

• Nutritional deficiencies may cause indigestion. Diets which are low in pantothenic acid (vitamin B5) or other vitamins can lead to indigestion.

On the other hand, taking large doses of certain vitamins can cause indigestion. Taking vitamin E in doses larger than the Recommended Daily Dietary Allowance (RDA) can cause indigestion. Vitamin supplements should always be taken on a full stomach to avoid irritation of the stomach lining. Vitamin supplements in doses larger than the RDA should be avoided if they cause indigestion.

• Drink lots of water.

• Avoid carbonated drinks since they usually contain acid.

• Use caution in taking chewable or liquid antacids, since their frequent use can cause the stomach to actually produce more acid.

• Folk medicine remedies for indigestion include:

> Eating alfalfa sprouts, slices of raw potato or raw turnip to relieve indigestion.

> Camomile tea, made from the camomile herb, is an old folk remedy for indigestion that is worth trying, says Varro E. Tyler, Ph.D., dean of the Schools of Pharmacy, Nursing and Health Sciences at Purdue University. Boil half an ounce of camomile in 1-1/2 cups of water. Let it sit for at least ten minutes to get the most out of the herb, he suggests. Take a few sips of the tea, several times each day as needed.

• Another herb recommended by Dr. Tyler for indigestion is capsicum. Capsicum is commonly known as chili pepper. While some may think that chili pepper causes more indigestion than it helps, Dr. Tyler disagrees. Only a very small amount of capsicum, less than 60 milligrams, is necessary to help relieve an upset stomach, he says. Capsicum can also be used to relieve stomach pain, flatulence (gas), diarrhea, cramps and muscle aches, according to Tyler.

• Many cases of heartburn and indigestion are caused by yeast but remain undiagnosed, says Dr. Sherry A. Rogers of Syracuse, New York. She says that a yeast-free, sugar-free diet can help relieve the digestive problems caused by yeast.

Insomnia

Commonly prescribed drugs, stimulants, and the way we live can cause insomnia. Here are some of the usual causes of insomnia, cited by the Harvard Medical School Health Letter:

• Lack of routine sleeping habits (inconsistent bed times or waking times).

• Emotional crisis (work-related problems, loss of money, marital problems, etc.).

• Being over-aroused. Worrying about tomorrow's activities or planning events, while trying to sleep, is not productive. Perfectionists often suffer from this type of insomnia because they keep reviewing details in their mind, rather than relaxing and preparing for sleep.

• Lack of exercise or daily activities. Unemployment or physical inabilities due to age or disease may limit daily activities.

• Caffeine. Avoid all sources including coffee, tea, chocolate, soft drinks, and some prescription and over-the-counter drugs. Ask your pharmacist for a complete list of drugs that contain caffeine.

• Developing a tolerance to sleeping pills.

• Alcohol.

• Over-the-counter diet pills (most contain stimulants).

• Certain prescription drugs including:
  — asthma drugs.
  — blood-pressure reducing drugs.
  — heart-rhythm regulating drugs (anti-arrhythmics).
  — hormones, like estrogen, progestin, oral contraceptives, and adrenal hormones.
  — steroids.
  — levodopa and other drugs used to treat Parkinson's disease.

• Being bored or lacking a purpose in life.

• Depression.

• Naps taken during the day.

- Breathing problems that interrupt normal sleep.
- Nervous system diseases affecting the brain, spinal cord or nerves.
- Severe pain, fever or itching that disturbs sleep.
- Gland problems involving the thyroid gland, parathyroid gland, ovaries, testes, pituitary gland, adrenal gland, or the pancreas.
- Illegal drugs like marijuana or cocaine.

Fresh air in the bedroom may help alleviate insomnia. Opening the windows wide for about 10 minutes, then leaving them open about an inch, can provide a good supply of oxygen and fresh air for the night's sleep. A stuffy room may inhibit your ability to sleep, according to Dr. Charles Wolfe, Jr. of the Sleep Disorder Center in Chicago, Illinois.

Creating your perfect environment for sleeping can be helpful, according to the Mayo Clinic Health Letter. Fresh air, a cool room temperature, total darkness, quietness, and clean bedsheets may be conducive to a good sleep.

If you are in a situation where complete silence is impossible to achieve, try masking the sounds. A small air-conditioning unit, a fan, stereo or low radio may block out annoying sounds and create a constant environment for sleeping.

Don't get physically or mentally excited in the evenings. Don't exercise at night. Avoid sex just before bedtime if it leaves you in an excited state. However, some people find sex a release. They may find it easier to sleep right after sex.

A warm bath may be helpful to induce sleep. Dr. Peter J. Steincrohn says warm or hot water will raise the body temperature and increase tiredness. Warm water also helps to reduce tension and helps the mind to concentrate on peaceful things which should make it easier to fall asleep after the bath.

A plain ol' glass of warm milk may help. This is an old folk remedy that seems to have scientific basis to help insomnia. Dr. Ernest Hartmann in Boston has shown that L-tryptophan, an amino acid found in milk, helps people get to sleep more easily. According to Dr. Hartmann's research, L-tryptophan stimulates the production of serotonin which is involved in the brain's sleep process. L-tryptophan supplements are available in some places. However, we do not recommend taking these supplements because other research has shown that L-tryptophan speeds the aging process. At this time, it seems that drinking warm milk is the best way to get the help of this amino acid. L-tryptophan is also found in other milk or dairy products, bananas, tuna, sardines (with bones), soybeans, and turkey.

Sleeping with the herb "hops" may help lull you to sleep, says Varro E. Tyler, Ph. D. Hops are known for their role in making beer but they also have a sedative effect, he explains. A few years ago, people who harvested hops were found to be sleepy and tired after just a little while of working in the fields. Their actions led to the discovery of hops as a sedative, according to Dr. Tyler, dean of the Schools of Pharmacy, Nursing and Health Sciences at Purdue University. For the best sedative effect, Dr. Tyler suggests putting some hops in a muslin or cloth bag and using the bag as a pillow.

Eat a lot of carbohydrates at your evening meal, the last food you eat before going to bed. Eating meals of carbohydrates rather than protein may help people relax and feel drowsy, according to research at Texas Tech University. Psychology professor Dr. Bonnie Spring measured the difference between carbohydrates and protein meals in 184 people. Proteins made the people feel tense but the carbohydrates relaxed the men and made the women feel drowsy.

Kidney Stones

The majority of kidney stones are formed by calcium oxalate clumping in the bases of the kidneys. Kidney stones are very uncomfortable and serious, but there are steps you can take to prevent their formation.

• Changes in diet can help many people avoid kidney stones, which tend to recur in susceptible people.

> Drink eight glasses of water or fluids each day.

> Avoid carbonated soft drinks. A research study from the University of Florida published in the Journal of Chronic Diseases (38:11) indicated that carbonated cola drinks containing sugar were the top drink used by men who suffered from kidney stones. Milk, water, tea, beer and coffee were also tested as the primary beverage for several groups, but they did not seem to be

associated with a higher incidence of kidney stones. The consumption of excessive phosphorus, which is present in large quantities in carbonated soft drinks, is known to drive calcium from the bones. This mineral imbalance may play a role in kidney stone formation.

> Eat a diet low in protein.

> Empty the bladder frequently and completely.

> Get adequate amounts of pyridoxine (vitamin B6) and magnesium in your diet or as supplements. Magnesium and pyridoxine have been used to limit or stop calcium oxalate clumping, which is a major cause of kidney stones. Taking supplements of 25 milligrams of pyridoxine per day may help prevent kidney stone occurrence or recurrence.

> People who know they have a tendency to produce kidney stones may want to avoid large doses of vitamin C. High doses of vitamin C may cause high levels of uric acid in the blood. Some studies, according to Vitamin Side Effects Revealed, indicate that large doses of vitamin C can create conditions which, theoretically, might increase the rate of kidney or urinary tract oxalate stone formation. However, other studies indicate that people who take large doses of vitamin C do not have an increase in the rate of stone formation.

• For people whose kidney stones are formed from calcium and oxalate, Dr. Steven Kanig, a medical professor at the University of New Mexico, recommends:

> Reducing the amount of calcium in the diet. Calcium is found in dairy products, leafy, green vegetables, salmon, and sardines.

> Reducing the amount of oxalate in the diet. Oxalate is a mineral found in spinach and other green, leafy vegetables, tea and chocolate.

• Kidney stones can be removed by surgery or, in most cases, they can be crushed without surgery by ultrasonic waves from a machine called a lithotripser. Many large medical centers now have lithotripsers.

Leg Cramps

• Leg cramps occur most often when the feet and toes are

pointed. If you are bothered by leg cramps, try sleeping on your side or make a special effort not to point your toes while sleeping.

• Leg cramps during the night may be alleviated by loosening the covers at the foot of the bed or by placing a small board at the foot of the bed. The board can be used to lift the covers off of the feet and remove that pressure on the toes that occurs when you sleep on your back. It is also useful if the feet are gently rested against the board.

• Sleeping on your back with a small pillow under your knees or loosely wrapping your legs in towels each night may help prevent the cramps. Some doctors recommend elevating the foot of your bed about nine inches to prevent leg cramps (Lancet 1:203).

• If you sleep on your stomach, try letting your feet hang over the bottom edge of the mattress. Your leg muscles will be stretched and relaxed which should reduce the incidence of nightly cramps.

• When leg cramps occur, stretching the legs may provide quick relief. While in bed, grab the toes and the ball of the foot and pull them forward until the cramps stop.

• Putting the feet into cold water may help relieve the cramps.

• Frequent exercising to stretch the calf muscle, by leaning forward and pressing up against a wall with your hands while keeping your heels on the floor, can help prevent leg cramps from occurring. Slowly stretch the calf muscles, at least three time each day, until the cramps stop occurring. Exercise these muscles often to keep the cramps from recurring.

• Many people find relief from leg cramps by blowing into a paper bag — or even into CUPPED hands — then closing the mouth and letting the air come back into the nose for a count of 10 or more. Don't stretch your legs after the breathing procedure. In most cases, even with repetitions, this procedure takes just a couple of minutes for quick relief.

• Quinine sulfate can relieve the pain of night leg cramps and help relax the leg muscles. It is available over-the-counter in Quintrol®, Q-Vel®, Legatrin® and as generic quinine sulfate. Follow package instructions carefully. Quinine should not be used by pregnant women. It can cause undesirable side effects like ringing in the ears, headaches or nausea.

• Vitamin E has been used to treat intermittent claudication, a condition caused by poor circulation which causes cramping and blood clot formation in the legs. Vitamin E has an anticoagulant effect which helps prevent the blood from clotting and causing cramps.

• Poor circulation in the legs leading to intermittent claudication can be caused when the arteries in the legs become clogged with fatty deposits. This is a serious condition. If the arteries in the legs are becoming restricted, the arteries leading to the heart may also be closing. Your doctor should be contacted for treatment. To help relieve leg pain associated with intermittent claudication:

> Stop smoking.
> Lose weight.
> Begin a regular exercise program approved by your doctor.
> Rest your legs regularly.
> Eat a low-fat, low-cholesterol diet.

• Leg pains can be especially dangerous in diabetics. A complete loss of the flow of blood could lead to amputation, so diabetics should SEE THEIR DOCTORS immediately if serious leg pain develops.

• People suffering from leg pains should try wearing a pedometer, according to Dr. Peter J. Steincrohn. A pedometer is a small device that is worn to see how many miles a person walks. It is sometimes used by people while hiking or walking for daily exercise. However, Dr. Steincrohn recommends using it to show how much walking people actually do in their daily routines. Many people, he believes, do far more than they realize. Often a person will go to his doctor complaining about leg pains. He will say and believe that he is inactive. By wearing a pedometer during a normal day's activities, they can have an accurate count that may surprise them and their doctors. Once the number of miles in a regular day has been calculated by the pedometer, if it's excessive, leg pains can be helped by reducing walking and increasing the time the legs are raised. Keep wearing the pedometer so you can judge whether you are eliminating enough walking.

Caution! Daily activity like walking usually is a great health benefit. Don't reduce your activity unless it's excessive or unless your doctor recommends it.

Lung Diseases

Quit smoking, or never start, to lower your risk of diseases that obstruct your breathing. Lung diseases like bronchitis and emphysema are often associated with smoking or other forms of air pollution. Some lung damage associated with smoking will not be repaired once a person quits, but quitting may prevent the disease from progressing any further.

Avoid pollution. Pollution over a city, like London and Los Angles, has been known to contain sulfur and nitrous dioxides which worsen cases of asthma, bronchitis and emphysema. Chemical air pollution, caused by occupational settings, can also contribute to lung diseases, according to the Harvard Medical School Health Letter. Welding fumes, cotton dust, some vapors from the production of plastic, gases from smelters, and even aerosol sprays used in the home, contribute to lung diseases, says the Harvard publication.

Drink plenty of water, at least eight glasses a day, to help liquefy the mucous secretions that can obstruct breathing.

Breathing exercises may also help restore easier breathing.

Memory Loss

• Choline is thought to improve memory in normal people. Although not proven, Alzheimer's disease, a disease affecting the memory in elderly people, may be slowed by supplementing the diet with lecithin which is composed of choline and inositol. Therefore, supplementing lecithin or choline in the diet may help improve the memory. The vitamin choline is naturally found in soybeans, eggs, fish, liver, wheat germ, green vegetables, peanuts, brewer's yeast and sunflower seeds. The vitamin inositol is naturally found in organ meats, yeast, beans, whole-grain products, peanuts and citrus fruits. Also see — **Alzheimer's Disease.**

• Although not proven, Alzheimer's disease may be slowed by supplementing the diet with lecithin. Choline and inositol manufacture lecithin in the body. Therefore, supplementing choline and inositol in the diet may help improve memory.

• Memory loss and mental confusion have been associated with a deficiency of thiamine (vitamin B1). Yeast, liver, whole-grain products, wheat, eggs, milk, nuts, potatoes, leafy green vegetables, kidney beans and seeds are natural sources of thiamine.

• Dr. Alexander Reeves, a Dartmouth University researcher, says that staying mentally active is the key to keeping a good memory. Reading, social events, and challenging your mental skills will help keep your memory in good working order.

Doing crossword puzzles and word games can help older people retain their sense of reasoning, according to researchers at the University of Washington. They discovered that memory and reasoning often suffered when the people's minds were not actively used. Crossword puzzles and word games help to challenge the mind and should be continued at any age.

• A proper diet, regular exercise, and regular checkups with your physician will help keep you in overall good health, including mental alertness.

• Remaining sexually active, even in old age, may be a key to a better memory, according to a study by Lar Nilsson, M.D. of Göteborg, Sweden. "A drop in memory capacity and intellectual ability" occurs when you become sexually inactive, reports Dr. Nilsson. A sexually active life is essential for a good memory and a healthy life, he concluded. However, cause and effect may not be proven by his study. Other studies have shown that people in celibate religous orders generally retain good intellects in advanced age when compared to the general population.

Whether a decline in sexual activity contributes to a decline in memory as people age, or whether both conditions are often caused by a decline in overall health and activity is a question which cannot be easily resolved.

Menopause

Menopause is a natural stage in a woman's life when she stops menstruating and is no longer able to give birth to children. Because the levels of hormones the body produces change, about

25% of all women experience very unpleasant symptoms during their menopause. This hormonal imbalance can cause different symptoms in different women, but often causes hot flashes, irritability, personality changes, unusual amounts of perspiration, dizziness, and skin sensations. As well as difficult symptoms, during menopause women can become more susceptible to many serious diseases like diabetes, osteoporosis, heart disease and high blood pressure. Special care should be taken before and during menopause to ensure continuing good health.

• Estrogen is a hormone produced naturally in each woman's body, but the amount produced decreases from the time the woman is in her late 20's or early 30's until it stops completely (known as menopause). If estrogen production is stopped suddenly, as after a hysterectomy in which the ovaries are removed, replacement therapy is especially important to restore the hormonal levels in the body.

Estrogen was hailed as a wonder drug in the 1960's and given to women in large doses. Then reports linked it to cancer. Researchers now believe that estrogen given in LOW doses (called estrogen replacement therapy or ERT) is very effective in leveling hormonal imbalances yet is still safe. According to the FDA, (U.S. Food and Drug Administration) estrogen treatment is safest for women who have had hysterectomies because estrogen treatment, over a long period of time, has been shown to increase the risk of cancer of the uterus.

A National Institutes of Health (NIH) study concluded that to lower the risk of heart disease, women should take estrogen during mid-life, especially during menopause. The death rate from heart disease in estrogen users was one-third the rate of that of women who did not take estrogen. However, conflicting reports published in the New England Journal of Medicine claim that estrogen therapy can increase the risk of heart disease.

A new skin patch that will allow estrogen to be given through the skin rather than with a pill, may reduce some of the unwanted side effects and risks of estrogen treatment. The skin patch (called Estraderm® by Ciba-Geigy) provides doses of estrogen similar to estrogen levels in a woman's body before menopause. And because the estrogen will enter the body through the skin, it will bypass the liver and reduce the possibilities of side effects. Many women with gallbladder or liver problems cannot presently take estrogen pills but may benefit from the skin patch method.

The FDA says that daily estrogen supplements taken after menopause are an effective way of slowing down or preventing osteoporosis. The National Institutes of Health (NIH) advisory panel says that estrogen helps the absorption and retention of calcium by the bones. When estrogen replacement therapy is started right after women stop menstruating, hip and wrist fractures can be reduced by as much as 60%, according to the NIH.

One study by Dr. Don Gambrell, Jr. at the Medical College of Georgia, concluded that estrogen given with progesterone may even protect women against breast cancer.

• Limiting caffeine and alcohol may help reduce the undesirable symptoms of menopause. Caffeine found in all products, like coffee, tea, chocolate and cola soft drinks, needs to be eliminated.

• Vitamin E has been used to ease the "hot flashes" and other uncomfortable side effects associated with menopause.

• Calcium intake should be increased during menopause to prevent osteoporosis.

• Smoking can also add to the risks of getting a serious disease during or after menopause. A woman should stop smoking at menopause if she hasn't stopped already.

• Some women suffer from vaginal dryness and uncomfortable intercourse during and after menopause. Many doctors advocate estrogen replacement therapy for this. Also, lubricants are available from pharmacies. They are very safe to use and can make intercourse more comfortable. Doctors recommend that women who have continued sexual activity will experience fewer problems with vaginal dryness.

• Many emotional problems, claimed to be caused by the "hormonal imbalance" of menopause, may have a more direct cause. According to doctors writing in Family Circle magazine (11/5/85), sometimes the physical problems of menopause contribute to the emotional problems. For example, hot flashes during the night can cause an interruption of sleep and consequent bad moods or depression the next day. Such mood changes are actually caused by the lack of sleep, not a hormonal change.

Therefore, treating the physical problems associated with menopause, like insomnia, hot flashes and sweating, helps lessen the emotional swings.

Nails

White spots on the fingernails, split nails, and soft nails that peel are often caused by a diet that is low in the mineral zinc. Zinc is found naturally in liver, seafood, dairy products, meat, eggs and whole-grain products.

Ridges or pits in nails may be caused by psoriasis, a common skin infection. Psoriasis can also cause toe-nails and fingernails to lose their shine or become discolored.

Brittle nails may be caused by a deficiency of iron, over-use of nail polish or nail-polish remover, or exposure to harsh chemicals or detergents, according to Paula Blake, R.N. in Bestways magazine. To improve the nails:

• Take better care of your hands and feet. Don't expose them to chemicals or detergents. Use rubber gloves when washing dishes or doing major cleaning.

• Eliminate nail polish. Allow your nails to "breathe" awhile.

• Try an iron supplement. According to a study done in Sheffield, England, many women with brittle nails simply have a low iron level. The supplement will often improve their nails as well as their energy levels!

• People with low-thyroid levels often have brittle nails. If you suspect a problem with your thyroid, discuss it with your doctor as soon as possible.

• Discoloration of the nails can be related to several different internal problems like breathing disorders, tuberculosis, cancer, and diabetes, especially in the elderly. If the toe-nails are yellow and the feet have small red patches on them, contact your doctor about the possibility of having diabetes.

• People with nails that break, crack, peel or chip may not be properly digesting their food, according to research by Johnathan Wright, M.D. Dr. Wright suggests that poor nails may be a sign that the stomach is not producing enough acid. Without sufficient acid, the body does not properly absorb the nutrition from the food that is eaten. Dr. Wright suggests taking betaine hydrochloride or glutamic hydrochloride with pepsin to increase the production of stomach acid. However, this solution will have to be continued indefinitely since the stomach will not produce more acid on its own.

Osteoporosis

Everyone loses bone mass as we grow older, but osteoporosis is an abnormal amount of bone loss — so much that the bones become brittle, the amount of bone mass is reduced, and the strength of the remaining bone is weakened. In severe cases bones become so fragile that even a hard sneeze could cause them to break.

Osteoporosis is often first noticed because of a fracture of the hip, wrist or vertebrae of the spine. Within three months of a hip fracture, 15% of elderly people will die, often because of blood clots that form in the legs during bed rest and then dislodge and travel to the lungs where they block vital blood circulation. Osteoporosis can also cause loss of height, a humped back (often called Dowager's hump) and extreme pain. Early osteoporosis is difficult to diagnose because you cannot notice the gradual loss of bone as it happens. Fractures or periodontal disease (gum disease) as a result of the deterioration of the jaw bone may be the first symptoms of osteoporosis.

Therefore, it is important to know who is at greatest risk for osteoporosis, what steps to take to prevent its development and what to do if it occurs. People at the greatest risk of losing their bone mass and developing osteoporosis are:

>   women
>   Caucasians
>   people with translucent or very fair skin
>   cigarette smokers
>   people with a slender build
>   people who suffer from anorexia nervosa, a drastic and serious loss of appetite
>   inactive people
>   women who are past menopause
>   people who consume large amounts of caffeine
>   people with family history of osteoporosis or hip fractures

>   people who have taken long-term treatment with steroid drugs for arthritis, asthma or other diseases

>   people who drink lots of soft drinks

>   people who eat high protein diets

>   people who consume large amounts of alcohol

Damage from osteoporosis is usually permanent. Lost bone cannot be easily replaced. Treatment includes heat, drugs for the pain, a back brace and rest. Rest, combined with moderate exercise like walking, helps keep the muscles in shape to support the weak bone structure.

Since damage from osteoporosis cannot be reversed, prevention should be a life-long goal. Women who have any of the risk factors listed above — any of them — should work actively to protect themselves against osteoporosis. It is often difficult to convince a woman before menopause that her lifestyle will affect the strength of her bones and the quality of her health after menopause — but it is essential. Some of the risk factors, like family history or individual bone structure are things we cannot change, but some things can be changed. The first step in prevention is to eliminate the unnecessary risks: quit smoking and reduce the intake of caffeine, soft drinks, meat, high protein foods and alcohol.

• Consuming adequate, but not excessive, calcium is the second most important step in prevention after estrogen supplementation in menopausal women, postmenopausal women and women who have had hysterectomies. Dr. Morris Notelovitz, M.D., Ph.D., author of Stand Tall, an excellent book on osteoporosis, recommends 800 - 1,000 milligrams of calcium daily for women prior to menopause and 1,200 to 1,400 milligrams for women after menopause. The best way to get daily calcium is from foods like milk, cheese, nuts, tofu and leafy, green vegetables. Three eight-ounce glasses of milk a day should supply your needs. If you don't like milk or need to supplement your diet, calcium carbonate is usually recommended. However, calcium carbonate may cause gas problems in some people, so calcium citrate, lactate or gluconate can be used.

It doesn't matter if the calcium source is oyster shells, "all-natural," or in a fancy bottle, as long as it is calcium. The important thing to watch is how much "elemental calcium" is

151

available. The least expensive generic brand of calcium is fine and will be the most cost effective. If you use calcium supplements, take them throughout the day, rather than all at once, so the calcium will be best absorbed by the body. Bonemeal is NOT recommended as a good source of calcium because its high lead content can cause liver or kidney damage.

Antacids like Tums®, which have only calcium carbonate as an active ingredient, are often cheaper than other calcium supplements. Although Tums® and some other antacids contain calcium, some doctors do not recommend using antacids for a daily calcium supplement because they may aggravate your digestive system.

People with kidney stones or kidney problems should NOT take calcium or increase their intake of calcium rich foods unless their physician agrees.

Many substances found in food, including oxalic acid (found in rhubarb and spinach), phosphorus (found in soft drinks and in many other foods), phytic acid (found in whole-grain products), as well as corticosteroid drugs (such as cortisone), dilantin, anticonvulsant drugs, tobacco, alcohol, caffeine or an excess amount of protein in the diet can interfere with calcium absorption or cause the body to need more calcium.

• Researchers at the University of Chicago Medical Center have discovered that glucose polymer, a type of sugar made from cornstarch, may help people absorb and retain more calcium. Although glucose polymer is now available in syrup or dried forms, more research is needed to discover its role in the prevention of osteoporosis.

• Taking more than the Recommended Daily Allowance (RDA) of phosphorus may drive calcium out of the bones. Excessive phosphorus in the diet contributes to osteoporosis and bone fractures. Soft drinks contain high amounts of phosphorus.

• Large doses of choline may cause excessive uptake of phosphorus which may deplete the bones of calcium. Therefore, large doses of choline may contribute to bone degeneration and increased fractures. If large doses of choline are taken, more calcium may be needed to maintain a proper calcium-phosphorous balance.

On the other hand, a deficiency of phosphorus, which often

occurs in people who regularly take aluminum-based antacids which bind phosphorus in the digestive tract so that the body can't absorb it, can draw phosphorous out of the bones and weaken them.

• Diets high in protein and low in lysine can contribute to osteoporosis. Decreasing the amount of meat and protein in the diet is recommended.

• Reduce the amount of caffeine, alcohol, salt, carbonated soft drinks and refined sugar in your diet.

Caffeinated-coffee drinkers lose twice as much calcium as people who drink decaffeinated coffee, reports Dr. Linda K. Massey at Washington State University. Caffeine causes calcium to be excreted in urine. Dr. Massey suggests that since many coffee drinkers are not getting enough calcium to begin with, drinking coffee containing caffeine is making their problem worse. Massey suggests that if you must drink coffee, drink decaffeinated coffee with lots of milk. The additional milk will help replace some of the calcium that the body needs (Prevention 39:5).

• Exercise helps prevent osteoporosis. Studies have shown that weight-bearing exercise helps the bones to grow stronger and more dense, so there is less chance of developing osteoporosis later on. Weight-bearing exercise is an activity, like aerobics, dancing, walking, jogging, rowing, hiking, rope jumping, tennis or bicycling in which the bones have to support body weight. Since the water supports the body while swimming, swimming is not a "weight-bearing" exercise. It is good for an aerobic work-out and developing muscle strength, but not for developing bone strength.

Exercise can even help strengthen the bones of older women, the Jewish Hospital in St. Louis reports. Until now, many experts believed that weight-bearing exercise could help prevent osteoporosis only before menopause. The new research shows that even women with osteoporosis who are past menopause can benefit from weight-bearing exercise combined with an adequate intake of calcium.

Women who have a very rigorous training schedule sometimes stop menstruating. This causes an increased risk for osteoporosis, since the hormone levels in the body are altered. Training should be modified so the menstrual cycle and hormonal balance is maintained.

• "Estrogen replacement is the single most effective means of preventing osteoporosis," writes Vivian Lewis, M.D. of the University of Illinois College of Medicine. Other studies including one by Linda S. Richelson, M.P.H. in the New England Journal of Medicine (311: 1273-5), have also explained that the loss of estrogen after menopause or removal of the ovaries, rather than the aging process, is responsible for most of the bone loss leading to osteoporosis in women. The FDA and the National Institutes of Health (NIH) advisory panel say that estrogen helps the absorption and retention of calcium by the bones. Minimal doses of estrogen and progestin seem to have the best results with the fewest side effects. Estrogen replacement therapy should start immediately at menopause, either natural menopause or surgical removal of the ovaries. When estrogen replacement therapy is started right after women stop menstruating, hip and wrist fractures can be reduced as much as 60%, according to the NIH.

Estrogen replacement therapy is only available by prescription and while under a physician's supervision. Estrogen should not be used, or should be used cautiously by women with heart disease, high blood pressure, endometriosis, asthma, epilepsy, diabetes, severe migraine headaches, gallstones, breast or uterine cancer, family history of cancer, or gallbladder problems.

• Vitamin D is needed to help the body properly use and absorb calcium. According to Dr. Lewis, only the U.S. Recommended Daily Allowance (RDA) of 200-400 International Units (I.U.) is required. Most people get enough vitamin D in sunshine and their regular diet. Vitamin D is also naturally found in fish, liver, eggs and artificially in fortified milk. Do not take excessive supplements of vitamin D because it can stay in the body for a long time and can cause side effects when taken in doses just larger than the RDA. However, the need for vitamin D increases as you grow older because the body does not absorb it as readily then.

• Magnesium is an essential mineral that works with calcium and phosphorus to form bone. Whole-grain products, vegetables, seafood and peanuts are good sources of magnesium. The U.S. Recommended Daily Allowance (RDA) of magnesium for adult women is 300 mg.

• Molybdenum is an often overlooked trace mineral which can help prevent osteoporosis. Unfortunately, it is often deficient in the American diet. Supplements containing 30 to 100 micrograms can supply enough for strong bones.

• Fluoride may help increase bone density. Studies are now underway at the Mayo Clinic in Rochester, Minnesota and other institutions to see what level of fluoride is the best for prevention of osteoporosis and how fluoride treatment may help the absorption of calcium and other necessary minerals. (Annals of Internal Medicine 98: 1013). However, fluoride may cause dangerous side effects, and supplementation should only be done under a doctor's supervision.

• Salmon calcitonin may be the best new therapy to prevent the loss of bone known as osteoporosis. Calcitonin is a natural hormone that helps bones develop in humans and other animals. Bone mineral content increased by 13% in women who were given calcitonin and calcium compared to women who received calcium and a placebo. Calcitonin could replace estrogen as the "treatment of choice" for osteoporosis because of its effectiveness and because calcitonin has fewer negative side effects than estrogen therapy, according to researcher Dr. Charles Chesnut from the University of Washington in Seattle.

• The trace mineral manganese may be an important element in preventing osteoporosis. Manganese is necessary for bone and cartilage formation. People with a deficiency of manganese suffer from poor growth of bone and cartilage.

According to an article in Bestways magazine and research in Science News (130:199,1986), basketball star Bill Walton developed osteoporosis even though he was getting plenty of calcium, magnesium and B-vitamins. However, Walton's manganese level was non-existent. Walton's bones got stronger with manganese supplementation. Walton was treated with manganese by his physician, Dr. Saltman, after his research revealed that the bones of rats who were put on a manganese-free diet became very brittle.

One problem in fighting osteoporosis is that calcium, an essential mineral in the development of strong bones, reduces the availability of usable manganese in the body. Many women who are trying to prevent osteoporosis are consuming foods and supplements that are rich in calcium. By doing this, they may thus be depleting their manganese levels. Natural sources of manganese are whole-grain products, fruits (especially bananas), vegetables (especially legumes), liver, other organ meats and eggs.

• Being safety conscious may help prevent undue stress and strain on the joints, especially for a woman past menopause with any of the risk factors for osteoporosis. Wearing low-heeled shoes, avoiding hazardous weather conditions and simply being careful may help prevent the fractures of osteoporosis from occurring.

Pain

Individuals feel pain differently according to Dr. Arthur Barsky, an assistant psychiatry professor at Harvard Medical School. Dr. Barsky says that circumstances, attribution, attention and mood affect how each person feels pain. For example, soldiers wounded during World War II felt less pain from their injuries than people in the United States who had received the same wounds. Because the soldiers felt they had received the wounds while defending their country, their pain didn't seem as great. Although we can't usually affect the circumstances that cause pain, Dr. Barsky points out that we can alter our approach to pain. Pain does not seem as severe if we remain calm and avoid becoming very anxious or depressed.

Pain can be a consequence of many diseases and health problems. It can be a warning sign to seek medical help or to take steps to relieve the pain. If pain isn't diagnosed as being caused by a serious disease, it can be combated in many ways.

Dr. Arnold Fox of the University of California at Irvine claims that an amino acid can reduce pain in about 80 percent of the general population. The amino acid is DLPA, short for DL-phenylalanine, that is available in many health food stores and drugstores. Dr. Fox recommends 375 to 400 milligrams of DLPA with each meal to reduce the pain of arthritis, migraine headaches, back problems, and depression. DLPA has no known side effects and seems to work by stimulating the body's hormones to block the pain signals from the brain, according to the doctor.

L-tryptophan, an amino acid which is sold in health food stores and in vitamin and mineral sections of supermarkets or drug stores, also seems to be an effective pain reliever in recent studies. L-tryptophan seems to increase the body's production of substances in the brain which act on the brain's pleasure-pain center to lower pain signals coming from the body.

Recent studies indicate that L-tryptophan is not particularly effective against headache pain, but it may help reduce the discomfort of chronic backache and leg pain. It is hard to evaluate how much influence the "placebo" effect may have on reported pain reduction in people who take L-tryptophan.

The higher your blood sugar, the less able you are to tolerate pain, according to research at the University of Minnesota College of Medicine, published in The American Journal of Medicine (77: 79). Since diabetics are struggling to keep their blood-sugar levels low, this is an especially important discovery for them. Generally, diabetics were found to have a lower tolerance for pain than non-diabetics. Other studies have shown that high blood-sugar levels reduce the effect of narcotic drugs prescribed for pain. Keeping blood sugar counts at low, acceptable levels will help diabetics to better tolerate pain.

Pressure Sores

• Pressure sores or bed sores are caused when a person must lie in bed for long periods of time. Patients recuperating from a serious illness or accident are most likely to develop them. Sores develop on the areas where the body has the most pressure. In their initial stages, bed sores are just annoying, but left unnoticed or untreated they can become very serious problems that jeopardize overall health.

• Application of cod liver oil, castor oil, granulated sugar, ice packs, linseed oil, cornstarch, egg whites or honey has been suggested for home treatment of bed sores. Unfortunately, none of these methods has been medically proven to be effective. In fact, some of these remedies may promote yeast or bacterial infections of the sores. The best treatment for bed sores is to remove the pressure on the area and treat the sore with antibiotic ointment.

• Prevention is much better than trying to find a suitable treatment. Take steps to prevent bed sores from occurring. A person who must stay in bed for several days should be turned at least every two hours. Use a water mattress, air bed, air mattress, foam rubber mat or a sheepskin pad to help reduce the occurrence of pressure sores. Bed sheets should be kept loose, and the person should be kept dry. Excess sweating or incontinence increases the chances of pressure sores developing. Never raise the head of the bed because this causes additional pressure on the lower part of the body.

Seborrheic Keratoses — see: Skin Problems

Senility

• Senility is not something that naturally occurs just "due to old age". Senility is memory loss, disorientation, confusion and loss of reasoning ability. There is a difference between the natural slowing of our reaction time with advancing age and being senile. Only about five percent of older Americans suffer from true senility. Most actual cases of senility are caused by Alzheimer's disease or damage to the brain caused by strokes. This senility is irreversible. Refer to the section on **Alzheimer's Disease** for a thorough discussion of that problem.

• However, many types of false senility can be reversed if the cause of the senility is discovered. Gallstones, alcoholism, undiagnosed infections, drugs, depression, dehydration, vitamin deficiency, and heart disease can all cause reversible senility.

• An untreated physical disease can also cause symptoms of senility. If a doctor dismisses senility as just a symptom of "old age," a serious physical problem like an infection, a blood clot or even alcoholism, could go untreated.

• According to the Harvard Medical School Health Letter, misuse of prescription and non-prescription drugs is the number one cause of unnecessary senility. People on continuous medication often:
> Forget whether or not they have taken their pills.
> Forget to take their medicine at the proper times.

> Have several different prescriptions which have been prescribed by various specialists who do not know about other prescriptions.

> Take over-the-counter medicines and vitamins without considering the interactions those drugs may have with their prescription drugs.

Doctors and pharmacists need to carefully monitor ALL DRUG USE, especially in the senile or elderly, to ensure against the unintentional misuse of drugs.

• These suggestions, including some from the Journal of the American Medical Association (JAMA), can help prevent apparent senility caused by drugs:

> Inform your doctor(s) and pharmacist of any medication you are already taking including all prescription drugs, daily vitamin or mineral supplements, and any non-prescription drugs (aspirin, acetaminophen, ibuprofen, cold medicines, laxatives) that you take regularly. Many drugs interact with each other. Some drugs can lose or gain potency and cause serious side effects if they are taken together.

> Use only one pharmacist. If you have more than one doctor, perhaps a family doctor, plus a heart specialist and a gynecologist, the pharmacist will be able to keep track of all prescriptions and alert you and your doctors to any possible problems. Be sure this pharmacist also knows about any regular non-prescription drugs that you use.

> Keep track of any side effects you may experience while taking prescription drugs and report them to your doctor. Loss of memory may be a specific side effect of a drug you are taking. If you can tell your doctor about side effects you have noticed, perhaps similar drugs without those side effects could be prescribed.

> Do not drink alcohol while taking any medication, prescription or over-the-counter, unless you have your doctor's approval. Alcohol may cause serious interactions with some drugs or increase the side effects of drugs that mimic senility.

> If you have a complex timetable to take your drugs, or if you must take several different drugs, make a checklist so you can be sure what drugs you should take and when.

> Keep each prescription in the original container that the

pharmacist supplies. Some pills have to be protected from light or air. The container will protect the pills and give you the name of the drug and the daily schedule for taking the drug. Do NOT use containers with different compartments for each day unless your doctor agrees. Storing different drugs together in the same container can create chemical reactions and changes. The drugs can form harmful substances or become inactive. Also, when drugs are combined in the same container, some people forget which pill is which.

> Always follow the label instructions. There are good reasons why some medicine is to be taken with food, needs to be refrigerated or needs to be shaken well before using. If you don't follow these instructions, your medicine may be useless or even harmful to you. If the instructions are not clear to you, ask your doctor or pharmacist. Get them to give you all instructions in writing so it will be easier to recall later on.

> Never take drugs prescribed for someone else. Drugs are prescribed on the basis of other drugs being taken, one's age, weight, health history and other factors. Exchanging medicine is extremely dangerous.

> Take ALL of your prescribed medicine, unless your doctor tells you otherwise. Just because you feel better doesn't mean you are completely well. Some medicine is prescribed to prevent problems, like high blood pressure, so you must take it as prescribed, no matter how well you feel. If you really feel that the drug is no longer helping you, discuss it with your doctor. NEVER stop taking a prescription without your doctor's approval.

• Depression that is not recognized or diagnosed is the second leading cause of reversible senility, explains the Harvard Medical School Health Letter. Some of the most common symptoms of depression include insomnia, decreased appetite, restlessness, anxiety, and feelings of hopelessness. Depression has been called the most common undiagnosed problem in the elderly. Many times the symptoms of senility like loss of memory and deterioration of mental capabilities are just shrugged off as "old age". If the depression is not treated the symptoms of senility will just continue and the person will get worse. However, if depression is properly diagnosed, therapy, including antidepressant medication, could restore the person to good health.

- Keeping mentally active will help deter the loss of memory. Reading, playing games, joining a discussion or tour group, becoming a volunteer, or any other mentally challenging activities will help maintain mental clarity.

Also see: **Alzheimer's Disease** and **Memory Loss.**

Sex Drive

Reduced sex drive often occurs with the normal hormonal changes which accompany aging.

Lack of estrogen after menopause may cause dryness in the vagina which makes intercourse uncomfortable. Lubricants, which are available without a prescription, are a safe and inexpensive way to reduce the discomfort. Estrogen supplements may help restore normal sexual activity to post menopausal women.

Certain vitamins, taken to excess, may interfere with the sex drive. Vitamin D overdose may cause decreased sex drive. Reduced sexual function may be caused by overdoses of vitamin E.

Many prescription drugs, including blood pressure medication such as Inderal® (propranolol) and Lopressor® (metoproprolol), may have as a side effect a decreased sex drive. Be sure to discuss with your doctor any problems you may be having. Often he will be able to change to another medication that will not affect your sex drive.

Doctors in the Soviet Union have linked an active sex life to a longer life. They also claim a direct correlation between being sexually active and avoiding disease.

Also see: **Impotence.**

Skin Problems

Age is often judged by the condition of the skin. If it is smooth and elastic, the person is assumed to be young. But if it is wrinkled and leathery, the person is assumed to be old. Our face and hands are the first to be affected by factors which age the skin.

- The chief causes of excessive skin wrinkling are smoking, exposure to sunlight, and reduced hormone levels, especially in women after menopause when estrogen levels drop dramatically.

> Most smokers have heavily wrinkled skin that looks twenty years older than natural age would indicate. Giving up smoking can restore much of the vitality and elasticity to skin in ex-smokers.

> Excessive exposure to the sun from sun bathing, working or playing sports in the sun without protection causes the skin to become tanned and leathery. Wearing hats and other protective clothing and covering unprotected areas with sunscreens can protect the skin.

> Women who have had hysterectomies, or who are in or beyond menopause, may discover that their prescribed hormone supplements keep their skin looking youthful.

• *Dry, itchy skin* plagues many older people. With aging, the skin often becomes dry as the oil glands produce less. To prevent over-drying the skin in winter, try to take fewer baths and more showers. If possible, take your bath or shower just before bed rather than in the morning. An evening bath will give your body the whole night to naturally replace the body's own oils and moisturizers.

Cleansing with soap in a long hot bath, actually makes the problem worse. Bathe, shower and wash in cool water to keep your skin moist. The U.S. Pharmacist (13-12: 24) suggests soaking in warm water for about ten minutes when bathing. This will allow the water to penetrate deep into the skin. After drying thoroughly, apply cream or ointment, which will act as a barrier to keep in moisture that has just been absorbed by the skin. The skin should be gently, but thoroughly, dried by patting with a towel, not rubbing. If the skin is still wet on the surface, the lotion will not be able to provide complete protection. Moisturize your feet, toes and toe cuticles to help keep your feet from cracking and drying.

The Food and Drug Administration (FDA)'s Division of Cosmetic Technology says that moisturizers with exotic names like placental extracts, collagen or elastin are no more effective than grape seed oil, squalene (shark liver oil) or geranium oil. There is NOT ONE PRODUCT that can prevent or reverse the effects of aging, according to the FDA. Rather than expensive creams and store-made moisturizers, many models use nothing but food shortening to keep their skin soft and smooth.

Use a soap containing glycerin to keep your skin from drying. Bath oils make your skin feel good, but they make the tub very slippery which is dangerous. Also it's good to use a non-irritating soap that contains a moisturizer rather than a "pure" soap. Avoid using any gel or lotion that contains alcohol because it will dry out the skin. Do not use bubble bath. According to the U.S. Food and Drug Administration (FDA), "Excessive use (of bubble bath) or prolonged exposure may cause irritation to skin and urinary tract. Discontinue use if rash, redness or itching occurs."

If you suffer from dry skin or eczema, dress lightly to avoid sweating. Perspiring increases dry skin problems. Do not wear clothes made from wool or silk because these materials can aggravate dry skin. Whatever you do, DO NOT SCRATCH! Scratching will only irritate the skin and make the condition worse.

Many people with dry skin problems wear rubber gloves when doing dishes and other chores to "protect" their hands. However, the chemicals in rubber gloves often bother people with sensitive skin according to the journal Contact Dermatitis (14:20). Plastic gloves are a better choice. If possible, buy plastic gloves that are too large and wear a pair of cotton gloves underneath. The cotton gloves will help absorb the sweat and protect your skin.

Psoriasis, a chronic skin disease that causes scaly red patches of skin on the arms, elbows, scalp, knees, legs, and other parts of the body, may be reduced by cutting arachidonic acid (AA) out of the diet. Arachidonic acid (AA) is found in meat, eggs, poultry and dairy products and has been found to cause the patches of psoriasis to turn red and swell according to the journal CUTIS (34: 497). It is recommended that people suffering from psoriasis try a diet of fruit, vegetables, bread and other cereal products, and fish, to lessen the occurrences of psoriasis. Fish oil capsules are also reported to help neutralize the AA found in our diets.

Dry skin is extremely noticeable in the winter months when the air within the home is usually very dry. Adding a cool-air humidifier to your home will help. Also, growing plants that require a lot of water, like ferns, large-leaved plants like begonias and bamboo will help because they give off moisture! Try placing some of these plants in your bedroom and around the house to add extra moisture to the air.

163

- To help end dry skin:

> Drink eight glasses of water a day. The water will benefit your entire body, including keeping your skin moist, preventing dehydration, and helping to flush out waste materials.

> Do not overbathe. Shower or bathe only every second day. Between baths, try a sponge bath to clean under your arms, your rectum and your pubic area, which need to be cleaned daily. Excessive showering dries out the skin unnecessarily.

> Use cool or lukewarm water. Hot water dries out the skin more than cool water.

> Avoid heavily scented soaps. Fragrances can contribute to overly dry skin.

> For best results, prepare your skin before using a moisturizer. Allow your pores to open up by putting a towel dampened with warm water on your skin for five minutes. Then apply your moisturizer. Your skin will be more receptive to the moisturizer after the warm towel treatment.

> For a simple, inexpensive moisturizing treatment, apply a layer of petroleum jelly or shortening, then cover the area with plastic wrap for several hours.

> Dr. Diana Bihova, a skin specialist who teaches at New York University Medical Center, recommends moisturizers that contain urea or lactic acid. Remember that the price of the moisturizer is not a reflection of how effective it will be. Check the labels.

> To avoid dry legs, Adrian Arpel recommends shaving with sunflower, peanut, almond or sesame oil rather than shaving cream.

- *Dry, cracked or blemished skin* can be a sign of vitamin C or vitamin A deficiency. Vitamin A maintains the smoothness, health and functioning of the skin and areas of the body related to the skin, such as the mucous membranes. Vitamin A also helps build body protein and promotes the growth of body tissues.

An extreme overdose of vitamin A can cause dry skin or peeling of the skin.

- *Oily skin* and hair may be reduced by lowering the amount of fats in your diet, according to Jackie Rogers of the Life Control Institute in Phillipsburg, New Jersey. To learn more about how to reduce the amount of fat in a daily diet, see our report on

Cholesterol Build-Up in this book.

• *Photosensitivity* is an exaggerated redness of the skin after brief sun exposure. Redness, swelling, hives, and itching are symptoms of this "sunlight sensitivity". If your skin is photosensitive, it usually reacts to the sun more quickly and severely than normal. Some drugs, including tetracyclines, thiazide diuretics, antidiabetics, oral contraceptives, antipsychotics, antidepressants, antihistamines, anticancer drugs, corticosteroids, and psoralens can actually cause photosensitivity. Non-drug products also can cause photosensitivity. Some of these include: coal tar products, coal tar dyes, musk fragrance, some perfumes and even some sunscreens.

• *Poor skin color and appearance* may be caused by zinc deficiency. Zinc aids the growth and repair of the body and helps the B vitamins work properly.

• *Age spots,* the little brown blemishes that often appear later in life, or freckles can be reduced or removed by a solution of lemon juice or buttermilk and oatmeal. Keep the solution on the skin for at least 10 minutes and repeat this procedure each day until the age spots fade.

Age spots may also be helped by pantothenic acid, vitamin B5. A biology professor at Mary Washington College in Virginia, Thomas L. Johnson, Ph.D., claims that daily supplements of pantothenic acid completely cleared age spots in just a few months. However, be careful when considering vitamin B5 supplements. These supplements can change the action of high blood-pressure and blood-thinning drugs. Cigarette smokers who take pantothenic acid may experience more premature skin wrinkling than smoking causes by itself. Pantothenic acid is found naturally in yeast, whole-grain products, liver, salmon, eggs, beans, seeds, peanuts, mushrooms, elderberries and citrus fruit. The best way to fight age spots is by avoiding exposure to the sun and sunlamps.

• *Skin Cancer and Aging.* The best way to protect your skin from disease and signs of aging is to avoid exposure to the sun. Skin cancer and little brown splotches known as aging spots are directly connected to the ultraviolet rays of the sun. People who spend a lot of time outdoors, especially sunbathers and those who use sun lamps, are at the highest risk of skin problems. You can lower your risk by ALWAYS using a sun screen, preferably with a SPF (sun protection factor) of 15 or higher, wearing protective sun glasses, hats, or visors while in the sun, avoiding direct sunlight between 10 a.m. and 2 p.m. each day, and by wearing long-sleeves if you are driving for long distances in the summer with a car window down. Sitting under an umbrella at the beach may protect you from direct sunlight, but the dangerous rays bounce off the sand and back under the umbrella. Even under an umbrella, you should still protect your skin.

• Exposure to ultraviolet rays is known to contribute to skin cancer, wrinkling, and early aging. With the gradual depletion of the ozone layer, the protective layer of the earth's atmosphere, and with the increasing popularity of sunbathing, doctors warn that the development of skin cancer is on the rise. In 1982, one out of every 250 people developed skin cancer. But by the year 2000, one out of every 90 will develop it, forecasts Dr. Darrel Rigel of the New York University Medical Center.

• Learn to protect your skin:

> Always use a sunscreen. The Food and Drug Administration explains that sunscreens rated with a SPF (sun protection factor) of 2-4 offer only minimal protection; 4-6 is moderate protection; 8-15 maximal; and over 15 is considered ultra protection. There is only a slight difference between the protective power of a 15 and a 23 SPF-rated lotion, so consumer advocates recommend 15 SPF.

> Apply the sunscreen on all exposed skin.

> The sunscreen is most effective if you apply it 15 minutes to an hour BEFORE exposing yourself to the sun. Putting on the sunscreen prior to exposure allows maximum protection because the chemicals have time to properly penetrate the skin.

> Use a sunscreen that contains PABA (para-aminobenzoic acid) because it helps to absorb the harmful rays.

> Re-apply sunscreen after swimming or getting wet with perspiration. Waterproof sunscreen products should protect you for at least 80 minutes of swimming or sweating. Water-resistant products should protect you for at least 30 minutes. But if you towel off after swimming or sweating, you will remove the screen. Re-apply sunscreen after using a towel.

> Remember that the sun's ultraviolet rays can penetrate

through three feet of water. If you are snorkeling, surfing, swimming, or participating in any water sports, be sure to wear a waterproof sunscreen. Even though you may not feel the heat while in the water, your skin could be severely damaged.

> Wear a hat.

> Wear sunglasses.

> If you are really sensitive to the sun, but you enjoy swimming, use a waterproof sunscreen and wear a dark T-shirt over your bathing suit while you are in the water. Re-apply the sunscreen after swimming, even if it is waterproof.

> Beware of increased exposure to ultraviolet rays when you are in high altitudes or places close to the equator.

> Doctors suggest that everyone, especially people who spend a lot of time outdoors in the sunshine or people who are fair-skinned, should regularly examine themselves for warning signs of skin cancer including: a change in the color or size of a wart or mole; a sore that will not heal or is slow to heal; or a thickening or lump in the breast, lip, tongue or elsewhere. Active sunbathers, farmers, lifeguards, outdoor construction workers and sailors need to be particularly careful.

> Dangerous exposure to ultraviolet rays is not limited to the summer months. Be careful when participating in winter sports like skiing, ice skating and snowmobiling because the sun's rays are reflected by the snow and exposure to them is intensified.

• As you get older you should wear less make-up, Vera Brown says. Since make-up accents wrinkles, Brown believes less make-up is more flattering to an older woman.

• Seborrheic keratoses are often called "the barnacles of aging" and are the most common noncancerous skin tumors that affect older white Americans. Seborrheic keratoses are brown or yellow raised spots with a greasy, scaly crust that most often appear on the shoulders, back and upper chest. They can be scraped off by a doctor.

• Puffy eyes and bags under the eyes can be relieved by placing slices of cold cucumbers or potatoes on the closed eyes. However, it seems that any kind of cold compress will work just as well. Some models place used tea bags on their eyes, because tea contains tannin that causes the skin to tighten up, but just temporarily. Tannin is thought to be a cancer-causing agent and can also stain the skin, so we cannot recommend tea bags. Sometimes puffy eyes in the morning can be caused by detergent in your bed sheets that is irritating your eyes. Try rinsing your sheets and pillow cases at least two extra times or switch to a mild detergent like Ivory®.

• Facial flushing can be eased by sucking on ice cubes, suggests Dr. Johnathon Wilkin at McGuire Veterans Hospital in Richmond, Virginia. Many people suffer facial flushing from drinking hot drinks, getting excited or angered, or from menopause. By sucking on ice cubes, the blood in the neck area is cooled and the flushing stops, Wilkin explains.

Also see: **Wrinkles.**

Sleep Problems — see: Insomnia

Smell, Loss of

Loss of smell can be a symptom of sinus infection or other serious disease that needs medical attention. It may also be a symptom of vitamin A or zinc deficiency. Liver, eggs and whole milk products are good food sources of vitamin A. Carotene, which is converted by the body into vitamin A, is found in fruits and vegetables, especially yellow vegetables such as carrots. Many vitamins are destroyed in cooking food, but carotene is released when vegetables are cooked. Thus, cooked vegetables are better sources of carotene than raw vegetables.

Liver, seafood, dairy products, meat and eggs are good sources of zinc. Vegetable products are poor sources of zinc. Whole wheat and other whole grain products contain zinc in a less available form than animal products.

Snoring

• Rolling a snorer onto his stomach or just changing his position may alleviate the problem. Sleeping on an extra pillow may help.

• Snoring can be aggravating to a sleeping partner, as well as harmful to the sleeper. Since many people snore only when they lie flat on their backs and their jaws drop open, try this simple suggestion. In the top of the snorer's pajamas, sew in a large fishing sinker, tennis ball, marble or other hard, large round object, as suggested by Southern Medical journal (79:161). The object should be sewn in so that if the snorer rolls onto his back, the annoying object will press onto the spine below the neck. The snorer will usually roll onto his side without waking up.

• If you wear dentures, keep them in all night to avoid snoring, says James Wasco, M.D. in Women's Day magazine (49:14). Dentures help keep the mouth in a natural position and may reduce bouts of snoring. Be careful, however; some people choke when sleeping with false teeth.

• Snoring is sometimes associated with sleep apnea, a dangerous problem occuring when someone temporarily stops breathing during sleep. According to the Food and Drug Administration (FDA), overweight men seem to suffer from sleep apnea more than any other group. People with short, thick necks also tend to suffer from sleep apnea. People with sleep apnea score about ten points lower than normal on IQ tests because the condition affects their ability to concentrate and remember, reports the journal Sleep (June 1987).

Loud snoring or severe snoring episodes associated with gaps in breathing should be reported to your doctor. If you suspect sleep apnea, do not take sleeping pills, tranquilizers, over-the-counter sleeping products or cold medicines as they could alter your body's ability to start breathing again. Sleep apnea can be fatal, so self-treatment is not recommended. Work with your doctor to overcome this problem.

Signs of sleep apnea which should be reported to your physician (FDA Consumer 20:10) include:

> not feeling awake or rested after sleeping
> snoring
> waking up breathless or with a snort in the middle of a sleepful period
> daytime sleepiness
> sleepwalking
> observation by another person that you stop breathing during your sleep
> hallucinations

> irritability
> bedwetting
> blackouts
> senility
> poor concentration
> loss of interest in sex
> personality changes
> irrational behavior
> morning headaches
• To relieve sleep apnea, your doctor may suggest:
> losing weight
> sleeping on two pillows
> raising the head of the bed by six inches
> sleeping in a reclining chair
> not sleeping on your back
> surgically removing the tonsils or adenoids
> using a Continuous Positive Airway Pressure (CPAP) device that must be prescribed by a doctor. This machine is attached to the nose of a person with sleep apnea and gently applies constant air pressure during the night so breathing will not be interrupted. According to the FDA, the device is effective in about 85% of sleep apnea patients.

Sores — see: **Pressure Sores**

Stroke Prevention
• Strokes are the third leading cause of death in the United States. A stroke occurs when a blood vessel in the brain ruptures or become blocked by a clot. Strokes are closely related to coronary heart disease and atherosclerosis, so things that help prevent them may also help prevent strokes.

Strokes are found more often in areas of the country where the water is soft; "soft" water contains few minerals other than sodium. The "stroke belt", close to the Atlantic coast in Georgia and South Carolina, is an area where the water is naturally soft. People who live in areas of the country where the water is hard, containing minerals such as calcium, magnesium and selenium, have lower rates of strokes. Adding these minerals to the diet in the form of mineral supplements or drinking low-sodium mineral water may help to prevent strokes in areas where the water is soft.

• Risk factors for stroke include smoking, being overweight, having high blood pressure, hardening of the arteries (arteriosclerosis), diabetes, meningitis, congenital heart disorders, sickle cell anemia, family history of heart disease or strokes, those over age 60 or women taking oral contraceptives are at an increased risk of suffering a stroke.

• You can take certain steps to reduce the risk of a stroke:

> Stop smoking. Smoking has been proven to increase the risk of stroke, reports The New England Journal of Medicine (315:717-20). After a person gives up smoking for at least five years, the risk of having a stroke will drop to about the same level as that of a nonsmoker.

> Lose weight.

> Get regular exercise.

> Control your blood pressure. Have your blood pressure monitored regularly and keep it below 140/90. Limit your intake of salt including salt-cured foods, especially if you are black. Many people, especially those with ancestors from warm regions, including almost all blacks have a "salt conservation gene" that makes them retain salt and water and have high blood pressure when dietary salt isn't low. The only way to combat this tendency is with a diet that is almost salt-free — less than one gram per day from all sources.

> Learn to manage your stress.

> Avoid alcohol. A study by researchers in Birmingham, England, showed that men with heavy alcohol consumption have an increased risk of stroke (The New England Journal of Medicine 315:1041-6). Alcohol raises blood pressure and counteracts the effects of exercise, according to a study from the Medical College of Wisconsin.

> Do not use illegal drugs. Use of cocaine, heroin and amphetamines has been linked to an increased risk of stroke.

> Eat well. Your diet should consist of low-cholesterol, low-fat foods. Also see: **Cholesterol Build-Up**.

Eating fresh fruit and vegetables daily could decrease your risk of having a stroke by up to 40%, according to a new study published in The New England Journal of Medicine 316:235-40). Potassium, found in many fruits and vegetables, may be the difference, say the researchers. Potassium helps lower blood pressure levels; high blood pressure is the leading factor in strokes. Potatoes, raisins, tomatoes, bananas, avocados, orange juice, apricots, squash and cantaloupe are all good sources of potassium.

> Keep diabetes in control. High blood sugar levels in diabetics increase the possibility of a stroke.

• If you are at high risk for a stroke, you may consider taking daily aspirin. Studies have shown than just a small amount of daily aspirin, as little as a child's aspirin or half a regular aspirin, may help to prevent strokes. DO NOT start this treatment without your doctor's consent because it is NOT considered standard medical practice at this time. Don't take a lot of aspirin. Aspirin can cause bleeding, especially if taken in large doses.

• Many people often suffer several small strokes without realizing that a stroke has occurred, according to Columbia University's Health and Nutrition newsletter. Without medical treatment, the strokes usually increase in severity. To prevent a fatal stroke it is important to recognize the early warning signs and get quick medical attention.

• Some of the signs of a small stroke identified by the American Heart Association are:

> Change in vision, like a flash of blindness or double vision.

> Difficulty with speech.

> Unexplained headaches or dizziness.

> Impaired judgment.

> Numbness, weakness or tingling sensations.

> Sudden change in mental abilities.

> Sudden change in personality.

> Any symptoms that seem to occur only on one side of the body.

Swelling In Feet and Legs

Swelling in the feet and legs may be a symptom of kidney disease or heart disease. Because these are serious problems, it is important to be seen by a doctor. Swelling in the feet and legs in women may be caused by hormonal imbalances, especially at the end of a woman's monthly cycle. Supplements of the pyridoxine (a B vitamin) and magnesium may help prevent premenstrual tension and bloating.

Taste — Loss of

Loss of taste is often closely related to loss of smell, especially in the elderly. The taste buds can distinguish sweetness, saltiness and bitterness, but finer distinctions of taste are related to the sense of smell.

• Zinc supplements may improve the sense of taste, according to Vitamin Side Effects Revealed. Anorexia nervosa, a serious loss of appetite, has been successfully treated with zinc supplements. High doses of zinc can be dangerous, but eating foods rich in zinc or taking 15 milligrams of zinc a day could improve the sense of taste. Liver, seafood, dairy products, meat and eggs are good natural sources of zinc.

• Long-term use of smokeless tobacco, like chewing tobacco and snuff, "may reduce taste sensitivity and . . . alter preferences for sweet, salty and bitter solutions," according to Dr. David J. Mela of the Monell Chemical Senses Center (The New England Journal of Medicine 316: 18, 1165-66).

Smoking can also cause problems with taste by damaging the tastebuds.

Teeth Grinding

Teeth grinding can lead to serious dental problems, including temporomandibular joint dysfunction (TMJ) and loss of teeth. It occurs more often as we age. Sometimes teeth clenching and grinding can be stopped by practicing relaxation techniques, but professional counseling may be necessary if the behavior is a result of deep tension or anxiety. See your doctor or dentist if you suspect that you grind your teeth during the night.

• Taking pantothenic acid (vitamin B5) is claimed to lower the incidence of teeth grinding during sleep.

Tiredness

Getting a good night's sleep is an important step to avoid being tired or suffering from tiredness or fatigue. Sleep on a comfortable bed; keep your room well-ventilated and at a comfortable temperature; and get between 8 - 10 hours of sleep each night depending on your individual preference. Also see: **Insomnia**.

Quit smoking. Not only can smoking cause hardening of the arteries and lung cancer, but it limits the amount of oxygen the blood can process. Since the blood cannot use the oxygen properly, smokers are more inclined to suffer from tiredness.

In some cases, fatigue can be helped by exercise. A brisk walk or swim before breakfast may really help overcome morning fatigue. The physical activity will help get the blood circulating and oxygen will be produced. The oxygen supply will help stimulate the whole body, including the brain. After the exercise, be sure to eat breakfast.

Tiredness may be caused by skipping or skimping on breakfast. According to a recent study, people suffering from fatigue and who had been skipping breakfast experienced less fatigue when they ate high protein breakfasts including meat, fish, cheese (mozzarella, provolone or cottage), or egg whites and two tablespoons of brewer's yeast.

Some people discover their fatigue is reduced if they eat smaller, yet more frequent meals throughout the day. Eating small portions of food, perhaps six times a day, seems to keep the body's energy at a constant level.

Have your eyes examined. Improper glasses or contacts can put great strain on your eyes and zap your energy. An eye exam may discover a visual problem that has been causing your tiredness.

Lose weight. Think of how much strain a 20 pound sack of potatoes would put on your body, then ask yourself if you are 20 pounds overweight. The extra pounds you carry just put additional stress and strain on your heart, circulation system and the whole body. The extra stress may not leave the body any excess energy and you would feel tired. Proper nutrition and good eating habits will help you lose weight, fight fatigue and improve your overall health.

Change your routine. Any tedious routine, at home or at work, can cause tiredness and feelings of depression. Try doing something spontaneously and change your daily schedule if possible. Just these changes may help reduce tiredness, fatigue and depression.

Extreme tiredness, combined with an intolerance to cold, weight gain and achy muscles, may be caused by a thyroid gland problem. The thyroid gland is located in your neck and produces a hormone called thyroxine that is essential for all the body's metabolic processes. If the thyroid gland doesn't produce enough hormones — called hypothyroidism, your body will start to slow down. Hypothyroidism is quite common and can easily be treated by prescription drugs. If you suspect this condition, visit your doctor as soon as possible.

Ulcers

• Stomach ulcers can occur for a variety of reasons. Ulcers are uncommon in people who eat a diet that contains a lot of dietary fiber, such as fiber found in whole grain products. Although whole grain products can't cure stomach ulcers, in many cases they can help prevent their recurrence once healed, according to a recent scientific study.

• Some doctors suggest taking an antacid every hour while awake as a treatment for ulcers, as well as once during the middle of the night. This treatment can be effective, but it is hard for patients to be completely faithful in doing something every hour on the hour. Also, most antacids are high in sodium content. Read labels carefully to find one with the lowest sodium.

• Ulcers can be irritated by not allowing enough time between eating and the time you lie down to go to sleep. Because all of your body functions slow down while you're sleeping, the stomach does not digest food quickly, and excessive acid is produced. To avoid irritating ulcers, doctors recommend that a person should not eat for two to three hours before going to sleep.

• People with ulcers should avoid foods which cause stomach pain. Meat, hot foods and drinks, spicy foods, acidic foods, and hard, fibrous foods, such as raw carrots or popcorn, may aggravate ulcers. Soft foods containing dietary fiber are usually well tolerated if the fiber is finely ground whole wheat flour, oat flour or oatmeal.

- People suffering with ulcers were formerly encouraged to drink milk to "coat" their stomachs before eating or going to bed. However, in the last few years, researchers have discovered that milk actually stimulates acid production, so it should be avoided by people with ulcers.

- Plantains, a type of banana commonly found in tropical countries, may help heal gastric ulcers, according to researchers. Raw plantains seem to stimulate the growth of new stomach cells which helps the ulcers heal, reports Ralph Best at the University of Aston in England. It seems that heat destroys the healing chemical, so Best recommends eating the plantain raw or cooked slowly at a low temperature.

- Smokers may find that their ulcers begin to heal when they quit smoking.

- Stomach ulcers can be treated quite successfully by three prescription drugs, Tagamet ®, Zantac® and Pepcid®. Zantac® and Pepcid® have fewer side effects than Tagamet®, but they are more expensive. All these drugs shut off the flow of stomach acid which irritates stomach ulcers and prevents them from healing. Healing usually takes places within a few weeks of taking one of these drugs.

- A study involving almost 200 patients in four countries showed that Maalox® Therapeutic Concentrate, taken twice daily, reduces recurrences of duodenal ulcers. Daily Maalox® was just two percent less effective than the prescription drug Tagamet®. Since Maalox® has few side effects and is available at much less cost than Tagamet®, this study could change ulcer treatment. The study results were presented at a recent meeting of the American College of Gastroenterology, and reported in USA Today.

- Stomach ulcers can be life-threatening, so they should be treated by a competent doctor. Do NOT rely on self treatment for this dangerous problem.

Urinary Incontinence
- Urinary leakage becomes more common as we grow older.

Leakage caused by simple movements like laughing, sneezing or sudden movement is called "stress incontinence". Incontinence can be annoying and embarrassing. It can become serious enough that the person cannot sleep through the night. In some cases, these problems are caused by a weak pelvic muscle, called the pubococcygeus or PC muscle, and can be cured by simple exercises.

PC exercises, sometimes called "Kegel" exercises, were developed in 1952 by Arnold Kegel, a gynecologist from the University of Southern California. He started the exercises as part of the recovery program from bladder surgery. Soon, Dr. Kegel discovered that the exercises alone often prevented the need for surgery.

Now, research has shown that by exercising the muscles for just 15 minutes each day many causes of urinary incontinence, urinary tract infections, and menstrual cramps can be reduced or cured. As a pleasant side effect, PC exercises increase the likelihood of a woman's experiencing orgasm during intercourse. PC exercises increase sexual endurance for men by 50%, according to Dr. William E. Hartman and Marilyn Fithian at the Center for Marital and Sexual Studies in Long Beach, California.

• PC EXERCISES — The most important thing about starting PC exercises is to locate and isolate the correct muscle. To locate the muscle, sit on the toilet and open your legs as far as possible. Try to stop the flow of urine by contracting the PC muscle. Relax the muscle, letting the urine flow, then stop and start the flow. In both men and women, the muscle that stops and starts the flow, is the pubococcygeus or PC muscle. Once you know what using the muscle feels like, you can exercise it when you are not urinating. This is the muscle that you want to exercise for fifteen minutes each day.

Four main exercises are recommended: "flicks" — contract and release the PC muscle to the time of a fast beat, like your heartbeat; "holds" — hold the PC muscle as tight as possible for 10 seconds, then release, then repeat; "bear downs" — bear down for three seconds, then release; "gradual holds" — gradually, to a slow count of ten, contract the PC muscle, then to another count of ten, slowly relax it. You may need to start slowly and build up to 15 minutes a day. Even though these exercises are simple, they could make the difference between good bladder control and lack of control.

- As well as the Kegel exercises, older people with urinary incontinence should remember to regularly empty their bladders, even if they don't feel the urge to do so. By emptying the bladder, you will avoid putting unnecessary pressure on the bladder and could avoid some control problems.

Urinary Tract Infections

Urinary tract infections should be treated under a physician's care and advice.

- Cranberry juice may be helpful in treating urinary tract infections, according to a study by Anthony E. Sobota published in The Journal of Urology. The research discovered that within one to three hours after people drink cranberry juice, they have an "anti-cling" substance present in the urinary tract. This substance makes it difficult for bacteria to cling to the walls of the urinary tract or to the bladder. Since the bacteria are not able to stay in the tract, the cranberry juice promotes faster relief from the infection. The "anti-cling" factor in the cranberry juice seems to work for up to 15 hours. Cranberry juice can often be used with other forms of treatment.

- If you suffer from urinary tract infections, do not use bubble bath. According to the U.S. Food and Drug Administration, "Excessive use (of bubble bath) or prolonged exposure may cause irritation to skin and urinary tract. Discontinue use if rash, redness or itching occurs."

Use of talcum or body powders in the genital area may also lead to urinary tract infections. Feminine hygiene sprays may also increase the risk of urinary tract infections.

- In some cases urinary tract infections are caused by a weak pelvic muscle, called the pubococcygeus or PC muscle, and can be cured by simple exercises. Research has shown, that by exercising the muscles for just 15 minutes each day urinary incontinence, urinary tract infections, and menstrual cramps can be reduced or cured. For complete information on how to perform these simple exercises, please see: **PC EXERCISES** — under **Urinary Incontinence**.

Varicose Veins

Varicose veins are greatly enlarged blood vessels, usually in the legs. Blood flow slows as it passes through varicose veins, and clots may form.

• Varicose veins are usually treated by doctors by prescribing support hose or surgical removal. Support hose, in most cases, may work as well as surgery and, of course, have fewer risks.

• The chief cause of varicose veins is a low-fiber diet which causes a hard stool. The resulting constipation exerts considerable pressure against the veins from the legs which pass through the abdominal cavity. The longer the transit time (time taken for food to be digested and excreted as feces) the more prolonged the pressure. This pressure makes valves in the veins, which prevent blood from flowing backward, open up and the veins balloon out.

Obesity and pregnancy can also cause varicose veins by increasing pressure on veins passing through the abdominal cavity.

Dr. Dennis Burkitt of the British Medical Research Council reported in the medical journal The Lancet on a large study of 1,000 people. His results showed that the greater the removal of fiber from the diet, the smaller the stool and the longer the transit time of food through the intestine.

The following are various studies relating to varicose veins from areas where people eat diets high in dietary fiber like bran, which is found in whole-grain products.

> Over a three-year period 11,462 patients were admitted to a hospital in the Zululand Reserve in South Africa. In addition, the hospital treated 103,857 outpatients. Of all of these, there were only three reported cases of varicose veins. (In a similar U.S. study, we'd expect to see well over 10,000 cases).

> A worker in another African hospital studied 30,000 outpatients and found only one case of varicosities.

> Dr. Burkitt personally examined 4,000 adults in Central Africa and detected only five cases of varicose veins.

> A questionnaire sent to doctors in 114 hospitals in Africa showed that 87% of the doctors estimated that they saw less than

five patients per year with varicose veins.

> Questionnaires sent to hospitals in India and Pakistan in areas where high-fiber diets are eaten indicated a similar low incidence of varicose veins.

It seems evident from such studies that a diet high in fiber may offer protection against varicose veins, whereas a diet low in fiber can be linked with a high percentage of varicose veins in a population.

• Varicose veins can be prevented or reduced by simple, natural changes in your lifestyle:
> eat a diet rich in fiber
> wear support hose
> raise or elevate the legs frequently
> don't cross your legs
> try not to stand or sit for long periods of time
> get plenty of exercise, especially exercise that uses the legs, like walking, jogging, swimming, dancing or cycling
> if you are overweight, lose weight
> avoid wearing tight shoes or boots
> consider learning and practicing foot massage.

• Crossing the legs may be an important reason why women suffer more frequently from varicose veins and blood clots than men do. Crossing the legs, especially at the thighs, impairs the flow of blood in the veins and arteries of the legs. When varicose veins or vascular disease is present, the slower blood flow may cause formation of blood clots. Clots can be deadly if they move to your lungs, heart or brain. Since women have been taught to cross their legs to be lady-like, it is a very difficult habit to break. Crossing your legs at the ankles is not as harmful as crossing them at the thighs, but should also be avoided if possible.

• Sitting for long periods of time, while recuperating, traveling or working, can also lead to formation of varicose veins and blood clots. Be sure to get up and walk around at least once every two hours to renew the circulation to your legs and feet. Rotate your feet and ankles whenever possible to improve circulation.

• If immediate family members have varicose veins, be especially careful to follow these instructions and try to prevent varicose veins from occurring, since a tendency towards varicose veins can be inherited.

Water Retention — see: **Fluid Retention**

Wrinkles
- Premature wrinkles can be prevented by good skin care:
> Do not smoke. A study published in the <u>British Medical Journal</u> showed that wrinkles around the eyes and lips, odd colored complexions, dry skin and leathery skin are more likely to occur in heavy smokers. Other studies have shown that the physical action of drawing in the smoke through pursed lips creates hollow cheeks. Smoking also decreases the circulation of blood which is necessary for healthy skin. A spokesperson for SmokEnders, a respected quit-smoking program, claims that if you quit smoking, your skin will improve.
> Avoid quick weight loss or gain. Sudden changes in body weight damage the elasticity of the skin and eventually cause wrinkles. Gradual weight loss or gain is better for your skin and entire body.
> Eat a healthful diet. Include foods rich in vitamins A, B, C, D, selenium and zinc for the most wrinkle-free skin.
> Exercise regularly. According to <u>Women's Day</u> (3/3/87), studies have shown that athletes' skin contains more collagen and is thicker than nonathletes. Collagen is an important factor in preventing wrinkles. Exercise is thought to help promote skin cell growth and improve the blood circulation.
> Don't strain or overuse your facial muscles. Wearing protective sunglasses can prevent unnecessary squinting. Corrective glasses may stop you from straining your eyes and facial muscles. Massage your facial muscles gently during intense periods of concentration.
> Practice stress reduction in your life. Stress can often affect facial muscle tension and cause wrinkles. Teach yourself to relax your facial muscles when dealing with stress. Learning to relax can improve the appearance of your skin.
> Avoid drastic changes in temperature. In extremely cold weather, expose as little skin as possible by wearing a scarf and

dressing properly.

> Avoid exposure to ultraviolet rays from the sun or artificial tanning lights.

> Do not sleep on your side or with your face on your pillow. Sleeping on your back will prevent your face from being pushed into your pillow which causes wrinkles.

> Moisturize your skin regularly. Nothing has been proven to actually stop your skin from aging, but moisturizers will help your skin to feel smooth and soft.

> Skin care experts recommend exfoliating your skin regularly. Exfoliating is the process where dead skin cells are removed, either with a commercial preparation (masks or scrubs) or by rubbing your face with a towel. Experts believe that exfoliating helps the skin to produce new cells which improves the skin's appearance.

> Wrinkled and sagging skin has been reported as a side effect of fluoride taken at, or above, the Recommended Dietary Allowance (RDA).

> Vitamin E supplementation may reduce skin wrinkles.

> To prevent wrinkles, we should watch the way we speak and the way we sleep, says Samuel Stegman, a dermatologist from San Francisco. When talking we often frown, tighten our lips and make other faces that help create wrinkles, Stegman says. He suggests placing a mirror by your telephone to see how you move your face, and so you can develop better facial control.

Also see: **Skin Problems.**

Precautions About Taking Prescription Drugs

As we grow older and experience many different ailments, we often take more drugs prescribed by our doctors. "People over 65 years of age make up 11 percent of the American population, yet they take 25 percent of all prescription drugs sold in this country", according to the U.S. Department of Health and Human Services.

Many studies are now underway to find a method that will ensure prescription drugs are given in the doses most effective for the patient's age. Special precautions should be used when older people take drugs. Research from the Baltimore Longitudinal Study of Aging shows that older people have less water in their body cells. With less water in the body, identical doses of the same drug taken by a young person and an older person would result in a higher concentration of the drug in the older person. In order to provide the best drugs for your problems, your doctor should consider your age. He may change your prescription dosage and the types of medication you receive.

Just as you should never take a prescription drug without a doctor's consent, you should never stop taking medication a doctor has prescribed without consulting your doctor. Serious problems can continue without proper medication, just as other problems can arise from discontinuing medication.

Take Your Medicine Correctly

Over one billion prescriptions are written by physicians every year, yet 78% of these prescriptions are **not** taken properly, according to the <u>Journal of the American Medical Association</u> (JAMA). Sometimes doctors do not take enough time to explain their instructions, but many patients disregard the instructions that they do receive. The following guidelines will help ensure that you get the best results from your medicine.

> Inform your doctor and pharmacist about all prescription drugs, any daily vitamin or mineral supplements, or nonprescription drugs (aspirin, cold medicines, laxatives) that you take regularly. Many drugs interact with each other and lose or

gain potency or cause serious side effects when taken together.

> Use only one pharmacy, preferably a pharmacy with computerized patient profiles with the ability to spot allergic reactions and interactions between medicines. If you have more than one doctor (general and gynecologist, for example) using a only one pharmacy will help you keep track of all prescriptions. Then, your pharmacy will double-check that you will take your prescription and nonprescription medication safely.

> Record any side effects you may experience while taking prescription drugs, and report them to your doctor.

> Do not drink alcohol while taking ANY medicine, unless you have your doctor's approval. Alcohol can cause serious interactions with some drugs and increase the side effects of many other drugs.

> Always follow label instructions. If there is a difference between your doctor's verbal instructions and the label instructions, contact your doctor immediately. There are good reasons why some medicine should be taken with food, kept refrigerated, or shaken well before using. If you don't follow the doctor's specific instructions, your medicine may be ineffective or harmful to you.

> Unless your doctor tells you otherwise, take ALL of the prescribed medicine. Just because you feel better doesn't mean you are completely well. Also, some medicine is prescribed to prevent certain problems. Whether your medicine is for prevention or to cure a specific disorder, always take it as directed.

> **Never** take drugs prescribed for someone else. Drugs should be prescribed after considering other drugs being taken, one's age, weight, health history and other important factors. Exchanging medicine is dangerous: don't do it!

The National Council on Patient Information and Education says that people ask too few questions about the drugs their doctors prescribe. If you learn more about your prescriptions, you can understand why you should take your drugs properly so they will be most effective. If you are well-informed about your treatment and condition you will know if something unusual occurs, and you will know when to contact your doctor for help.

Here are some guidelines from the Council of what to ask your doctor when medication is prescribed for you or someone in your family. Do not be afraid to write down your doctor's answers to these questions so you can refer to them later.

> What is the name of the drug?
> What is it supposed to do?
> How long will it take before it is effective?
> How am I supposed to take it?
> When am I supposed to take it?
> Are there any foods, drinks, other drugs or activities that I should avoid while taking this drug?
> What are the drug's side effects?
> What should I do if the side effects happen to me?
> Is written information available on this drug that I could have and understand?
> How can I get this written information?

Note: You can find the answers to questions about the good intended effects and bad side effects of your prescription drugs from a new book, **Prescription Drug Encyclopedia**. To get your copy, write the words "Send me **Prescription Drug Encyclopedia**" on a piece of paper and send it with a check for $9.95 plus $2.00 shipping and handling to: FC&A, Dept. PY-1, 103 Clover Green, Peachtree City, Ga. 30269.

Overdoses of Drugs

Whenever your physician prescribes a medicine for you, he has an intended purpose in mind and has designated a specific dosage of that drug for you. **Deadly** results can occur from taking more than the doctor prescribes. Do not try to "hurry up" the good effects of the medicine by increasing the recommended dose. Medicine takes a while to work within the body to bring about desired results. Give them time.

A Prescription List Could Save Your Life

Keep a list of all your current prescriptions in your wallet, billfold or purse. Include the name of the drug, what dose you are taking and the name of the doctor who prescribed it. When you visit your doctor (or doctors) have them check your list and keep it up to date. The list will remind them of your current prescriptions, and keeping it with you could help avoid dangerous drug interactions. During an emergency, the list will provide valuable information at the attending doctor's fingertips.

Some companies are now producing small cards, the size of credit cards, that contain a computer chip listing your important health information including current medical evalution, normal blood pressure, heart readings, and current prescriptions. In case of an emergency, the card could provide important information, and save your life. Ask your doctor or pharmacist how you can get one of these cards.

Making Medicine Easier to Swallow

For bitter tasting medicine, some doctors recommend sucking on an ice cube for a couple of minutes before taking the medicine. Then, your taste buds will be cold, and you won't notice the taste as much.

Standing, rather than sitting, while you are swallowing the medicine will help it work more quickly, some researchers report in the Clinical Pharmacology and Therapeutics journal.

Do not crush medicine unless you get approval from your doctor or pharmacist because crushing can alter the proper release of some drugs and reduce their effectiveness or inactivate them. Also check with your doctor or pharmacist about any foods into which you want to mix the crushed drugs. Some foods may react with the medicine, and you'll want to avoid those.

Storing Medications Correctly

People with several different prescriptions to take each day need ways to make it easier to store their drugs. Here are some important things to remember about how to store your prescription and over-the-counter drugs so they won't be harmed.

> Drugs should always be kept in the container the pharmacist supplies. Some pills must be protected from light, and some will be damaged by contact with air or moisture. If the bottle or container the pharmacist gives you is too large, just ask for another container that is more convenient for you. Don't store drugs in a pill box unless it's made by a drug manufacturer.

> Do not put different kinds of pills in the same container.

186

Putting different types of pills together can create harmful chemical reactions and changes in your drugs. (U.S Pharmacist 10,4:26). It is tempting to put your pills in little plastic boxes that have separate compartments for each day and different times — but if your pills become inactive, they will not do you any good. Also, when drugs are combined in the same container, people often forget which pill is which.

> Watch for changes in color, smell or consistency in your drugs. If you notice any such changes, take them to your pharmacist. He will be able to tell you whether they are still safe to take. For example, when aspirin develops a vinegary odor, it has probably lost its potency and should not be used.

> Watch the expiration date. This date is good only when the bottle **has not** been opened. Many drugs decompose when they are exposed to air. Once the seal is broken on a bottle, the expiration date is no longer in effect. Ask your pharmacist or doctor how long the drug will be good after the bottle is opened. Then, when you open it, write this down on the bottle as a new expiration date. For example, nitroglycerin (a blood-vessel enlarger) is potent for only three months after it has been exposed to air.

> If possible, avoid storing medicine in the bathroom. Since moisture and heat are the worst enemies of most drugs, the medicine cabinet in the family bathroom is not the best place to store them. The dampness from showers and baths can harm the potency of your drugs. Try to choose a safe, dry, cool place to store your prescription and nonprescription drugs.

> Use easy-to-open bottles. Many over-the-counter drugs come in child-proof containers that are sometimes "adult proof". Irving Rubin, editor of Pharmacy Times says, "Tamper-proof medication for children should not be tamper-proof for their grandparents". If you are sure that children will not be near your drugs, ask your pharmacist for a container that is easy to open.

> Keep all medicines out of reach of children. If you have children at home or if there will be little ones visiting your house, be sure to keep all drugs where the children will not be able to get to them.

> Dispose of all outdated and unused drugs by flushing them down the commode. In an emergency, family members may have

to locate and identify medications. Keep only current medications
on hand.

Protect Yourself Against Tampered Drugs

After well-publicized incidents of tampering with several
name-brand, non-prescription drugs, all consumers must learn to
protect themselves against being victims of drug tampering.

Although over-the-counter drugs have been carefully packaged
and are strictly regulated by the federal government, there is no
foolproof way to keep the drugs entirely safe. To protect you and
your family, follow these guidelines, recommended by the U.S.
Pharmacopoeial Convention:

Before You Buy:

> Consider what form the product that you are buying is
available in— and buy the form that is least likely to be sabotaged.
A tablet or caplet is more difficult to tamper with than capsules or
liquids.

While You're Buying:

> Carefully inspect the outer packaging of the product. Do
not purchase it if it looks at all unusual.

> Compare the box or container you choose with others of
the same product. Make sure there is nothing different about the
package you buy.

When Opening The Package:

> Watch for holes, tears, cracks or breaks in the outer
wrapping, cover or protective seal.

> Check to see if the outer covering has been changed,
unwrapped, or replaced.

> Read the lot number and information on the box or outer
covering, and make sure that it matches the information on the
product label or container.

> Inspect the shrinkband seal around the top of the container
to see if it has been stretched, distorted or opened and retaped.

> If it is an unsealed bottle, make sure the cap is on very
tightly.

> Check that the bottle is filled properly and not overfilled or
underfilled.

> Is there a seal in place?

> Look at the cotton plug or filler at the top of the container.

Make sure it hasn't been disturbed.

> Inspect the inside rim of the container for bits of paper or glue — this may mean that it formerly had a protective seal under the cap.

<u>While Taking The Medicine</u>:

> Make sure the color, smell, consistency and moistness of the product are what you are used to.

> Take the medicine in good lighting so you can double check that it has not been tampered with, and that it is the proper drug for your ailment.

Do not take any drug that doesn't seem just right. If you are suspicious about a drug or find any evidence of tampering, contact your local office of the FDA (Food and Drug Administration) or your pharmacist — right away.

Preparation for Surgery

Some medical problems will occur even with the best prevention and medical care. If surgery is necessary, proper preparation can aid your recovery, your finances and your peace of mind.

> Always get a second opinion for elective surgery. Some doctors will agree to do second opinions at a special rate. For the name of a doctor near you, who will provide an unbiased second opinion on your surgery, the Department of Health and Human Services has set up a toll-free hotline, 1-800-638-6833 or, if you live in Maryland, 1-800-638-1112.

Some insurance plans provide coverage for a second opinion. A growing number of insurance companies now insist upon a second opinion for elective surgery.

> Think positively about the operation and your recovery time. Talk to other people who have had a similar operation so you can be prepared for what to expect. However, keep in mind that everyone is different and your experience may vary somewhat. Write down any questions you may have and talk to the doctor about them before you go to the hospital. People who fear the operation usually have a more difficult recovery and suffer more discomfort, researchers from Vanderbilt University Medical Center report.

> If you can choose the hospital, investigate several hospitals before making a decision. Studies show that operations that are done infrequently have the highest risks so choose a physician and a hospital which have good "track records" and lots of experience with your operation. Make sure that the hospital you choose has done a minimum of 300 identical operations. You can get that information from their surgery department, local health office or peer review organization (PRO). The PRO is a committee set up according to government standards to ensure quality health care.

> You should also consider the size and type of hospital that you prefer. A large hospital that has a teaching facility, like a medical school, may allow many resident doctors still in training, to examine you and work on your case. On the positive side, resident doctors can usually call for help from many highly

qualified doctors in various specialties. These hospitals are usually the best prepared to handle emergencies and complicated treatments. A smaller hospital may offer more relaxed and personal care, but it may not have some of the technical capabilities or capable consultant physicians of a large facility. Visit the hospitals prior to surgery and choose the one that is best for your needs and wants.

> Discuss your admissions options with a hospital counselor during the week before your admission. You may be asked to choose between a private or semi-private room. Do you want a TV, a telephone, a non-smoking roommate, or a special diet? You may want to determine any extra charges for these options and check with your insurance company to see what they will cover before you are admitted.

> See if any of the admission or pre-surgery tests can be done by a local laboratory before you are admitted. This may cut your stay in the hospital. Watch out for unecessary repetition of tests. Your doctor may have recently done some of the tests, and the results could be transferred to the hospital to reduce expenses and needless repetition of tests, especially X-rays. Also, most insurance plans provide coverage for admissions testing done on an out-patient basis.

> Do not use any products containing aspirin within 48 hours of your planned surgery. Aspirin reduces the ability of the blood to clot, and this could cause dangerous excessive bleeding in surgery. Many over-the-counter products contain aspirin, including some: general pain relievers, cold medicines, back pain relief products, pills for menstrual cramps and products for upset stomachs. Be sure to check the list of ingredients before taking any medicine prior to surgery. If you are unsure about a product, ask your pharmacist or doctor.

> Do not take fish oil products prior to surgery because they also can increase bleeding time, reports The Medical Letter (29:731).

> Do not smoke within 24 hours before surgery because smoking "compounds the risks of anesthesia and surgery", according to doctors writing in the British Medical Journal 6/15/85). To avoid getting a respiratory disease after surgery, the doctors recommend not smoking for six weeks prior to surgery

and six weeks after the surgery.

> If you are overweight, lose weight. Additional pounds increase your risk of problems during surgery and recovery.

> Do eat a well-balanced diet as much as possible prior to surgery. Poor nutrition slows the healing process.

> Drink plenty of fluids, especially water, until they are restricted by the doctor. Dehydration, even in a mild form, may slow healing.

> Donate your own blood to the hospital a few weeks before the planned surgery. If a transfusion is needed during surgery, your own blood can be used to limit the possibilities of infections or reactions after transfusions. Check with your doctor or hospital about the procedures they prefer for donating your own blood.

> Once in the hospital, be sure you know the doctor in charge of your case and the nurses assigned to you. The nurses will be providing continuing care and they can be a good source of support for you.

> Check the wrist band that is placed on you during admission to the hospital. Make sure that everything is correct and alert a nurse immediately if anything is wrong. The wrist band is used to confirm a patient's identity and the type of operation to be performed, so it must be completely correct.

> Read any consent forms carefully before you sign them. If you are unsure about anything on the forms, ask questions before you sign. Do not allow anyone to force you into signing something you do not want to sign.

> During your stay, your doctor may check in on you only once a day. Remember, before visiting you he may have already read your chart of vital signs and may not need to examine you to find out how you are doing. Have your questions written down and ready to ask because you may not see the doctor again until the next day. If you need a lot of sleep for recovery, give your questions to a family member who would be present to ask for answers when the doctor arrives.

> Do not hesitate to ask questions. If you are unclear about any tests, procedures, or medications, ask your doctor or nurses. They will be able to explain why these are necessary and how you will benefit.

> Bring your doctor's phone number with you to the hospital

and give it to your immediate family members. If you miss seeing your doctor, you can call the office and leave a message for him or her to see you or call your family.

> Be sure to alert the staff to any drug allergies or other allergies you may have. If possible, before you take medicine in the hospital, check to be sure that it is the drug that has been prescribed. Be careful if a staff member seems to be careless.

> Exercise as much as possible. Bed rest makes the muscles weak. Walk as much as your doctor will allow. Try doing isometric exercises that push one muscle against another or against an immovable object like a bed rail. Exercise will help prevent fluid retention, bed sores, and blood clots while speeding your recovery.

> Try to be a pleasant patient. Remember that kindness usually begets kindness. Thank you's and support for your nurses and other caregivers will encourage them. At the same time, be sure to alert them to any problems or questions you may have.

Safety Tips To Avoid Accidents

By following good safety procedures you can help to avoid accidents. An accident that may have been minor at a younger age can cause many months of recuperation and hardship at a more advanced age. The National Saftey Council reports that older people suffer 23 percent of all accidental deaths, yet they make up only 11 percent of the American population. Try to prevent as many accidents as possible by doing these things:

> Keep your home in good repair.

> Take your time. Doing something in haste increases your risk of having a serious accident.

> Remove or tape down all throw rugs that could slip and slide.

> Keep stairways well lit.

> Install hand rails by all stairs and in your bathtub and shower area.

> Take precautions to prevent fires and use at least one fire detector on each floor of your home.

> Choose furniture coverings and drapes that are non-flammable or flame resistant.

> Don't smoke. If you do smoke, don't smoke in bed, after drinking alcohol or when you are sleepy.

> Plan your escape route in case of an emergency.

> Use one good dead bolt lock on each door so you won't get trapped in an emergency if you encounter several locks.

> Set your water heater thermostat fairly low so you won't be scalded by hot water.

> Avoid overexposure to the sun or to cold.

> Avoid unnecessary lifting.

> Always use a seat belt whenever you are in a vehicle. Most accidents happen close to home. Put your seat belt on even if you are traveling only a few blocks.

> Drive within the speed limit. If you have vision problems, avoid driving at night. Don't drive for long hours, during rush hours, or in bad winter weather.

> Never drink alcohol while taking a prescription or non-prescription drug unless you have your doctor's permission.

Don't drive if you have been drinking or if you are taking a prescription drug that dulls your senses.

> Learn cardiopulmonary resuscitation (CPR).

In Closing — Secrets For A Healthier Life

Take good care of yourself. This list of health tips has been compiled from reports in <u>Shape Magazine</u> and from the advice of several other health publications and experts:

> Have regular check ups by your doctor and dentist at least once a year and preferably every six months. Discuss your problems with your doctor. Remember that the best doctor in the world cannot help someone who will not tell him what is wrong. Find a doctor that you like ... someone that you can talk to ... someone that will talk to you, then trust him and follow his instructions.

> Stay trim. Keep your body weight within Metropolitan Life's ideal weight/height/body frame tables. For men, body fat should be limited to 14 percent. For women, 17 percent or less of body fat is good.

> Exercise at least three times a week for at least 30 minutes of aerobic activity like walking. "If exercise could be packed into a pill, it would be the single most widely prescribed, and beneficial, medicine in the Nation," said Robert N. Butler, M.D., the former Director of the National Institute on Aging. Regular exercise can improve heart and lung function, increase glucose (sugar) tolerance, and improve the rate that heart and muscle tissue use oxygen from the blood. If you have not been physically active, have a physical exam and get your doctor's permission before undertaking any new exercise program or strenuous physical activity.

> Keep your blood pressure under 140/90. You should know your own blood pressure and check it often.

> Keep your blood cholesterol levels low by good diet and exercise. Have your blood cholesterol level checked regularly.

> Give your body the fuel it needs for a healthful tomorrow. Doctors and nutritionists believe that a proper diet decreases your chances of getting cancer, diabetes, heart disease, osteoporosis or many other diseases. With a well-planned diet, someone who might die with a heart attack at 55, may extend his life by many years.

— Everyone, especially people over 65, should eat three

meals a day and avoid snacking. Even if the portions are small, it is best for your body to eat three meals a day.

— Be sure to eat a variety of fiber including fruit, miller's bran, vegetables, oat bran, whole-grain breads and cereals.

— At home or in a restaurant, try to eat foods that are lightly cooked: broiled, steamed, roasted or baked in their own juices. Raw fruit and vegetables are also good choices.

— Saturated fats, found in meats and dairy products, should be reduced to less than 10% of total calories. Foods rich in cholesterol that should be avoided or drastically limited in the diet are: egg yolks, organ meats, and most cheeses. Foods that should be greatly limited because they are high in saturated fats include: butter, bacon, beef, whole milk, cream, chocolate, almost any food of animal origin, hydrogenated vegetable shortenings, coconut oil and palm oil.

— Cut back on beef, lamb and pork. Never eat any of them more than three times per week.

— Unsaturated fats, such as fish and vegetable oils, may constitute as much as 10% of total calories. One of the best sources of polyunsaturated fats is in fish, especially cold water fish like salmon, trout, mackerel and cod. Researchers are discovering that fish oils actually lower levels of cholesterol and other blood fats associated with heart disease.

— Total fat intake should be less than 30% of your daily calories.

— Protein should constitute about 15% of your daily calories.

— Do not consume more than 100 milligrams of cholesterol for each 1,000 calories. Daily cholesterol should not exceed 300 milligrams.

— Reduce sodium intake to one gram per 1,000 calories Do not consume more than three grams of sodium in one day.

— Eat a wide variety of foods. Some foods are difficult to eat if you have missing teeth or dentures Even though eating raw fresh fruit and vegetables might not be possible, lightly cooking or steaming the fresh produce will still provide good nutrition.

— Since eating is often a social event in our society, it is sometimes difficult for an older person, who is alone, to keep proper eating habits. Try to dine with others whenever possible. Community meal programs in a church or social center are good settings for proper dining. But don't let your life center around eating. Develop other interests and goals. It seems that sometimes the only pleasure some people have is eating. Extra calories aren't needed or appreciated by your body. Remember the old saying — "don't live to eat; eat to live".

— Some people on fixed incomes do not eat properly because of financial constraints, but good nutrition does not have to be expensive. First of all, people on a limited budget should avoid eating out. But when eating out, try to enjoy the noontime meal. Noontime menus usually offer the same food at less expensive prices than evening meals.

When buying food to prepare at home, large quantities of staple sale items are often the best buy. If you do not have a freezer, try buying food in larger quantities and splitting your purchases with a friend. You'll both save money. Take advantage of coupons, special senior citizen discounts, and sales for the best bargains. Try to avoid buying prepared foods because they are usually more expensive. Eating less red meat and using fish and poultry will save you money and give you healthier sources of protein.

> Drink at least eight glasses of water each day. Water is necessary for regular bowel movements, to help prevent kidney stones, to protect us from disease, and to prevent dehydration. Many elderly people lose their sense of thirst, reports a recent study in the New England Journal of Medicine. According to the study, older people must be especially careful to drink eight glasses of water each day because they may not feel thirsty or uncomfortable. Drinking "hard" certified pure spring water is recommended. Author, Frank Cawood, prefers Mountain Valley Water. He says that, "it's low in sodium and has a good balance of necessary minerals like calcium and magnesium."

> Don't smoke. If you want to increase your chances of living longer and enjoying life more, you should not smoke or use tobacco in any form. Smoking has been linked to many life-shortening ailments like cancer, lung problems, osteoporosis and heart disease. It is never too late to stop smoking.

> Avoid alcohol. As you grow older, it is more difficult for your body to tolerate liquor.

> Women should do a monthly self-exam of their breasts and

have a yearly gynecological check-up, including a PAP smear. Women over 50 should have an annual mammogram (an X-ray of the breast tissue).

> Men should have a regular exam of their penis, testes and prostate.

> Be sure to get enough sleep. An average adult needs between 8 - 10 hours of sleep each night. You may also find a short afternoon nap refreshing.

> Your attitude towards life is one of the best qualities you can have to live a long and healthy life. Try to remain flexible. Don't be afraid to change as the world continues to change around you. Enjoy the pleasures of life by finding happiness in small things. Maintain your interests and develop new ones. Above all, think positive.

> Have faith. Our Lord sent His only Son, Jesus Christ, into this world to give us everlasting life. Jesus worked miracles over 2,000 years ago and still works miracles today. Your body may not always perform the way you would like, but with new life in Jesus your spirit can be healed. If you are interested in knowing more about new life in Jesus Christ, please write to: FC&A Publishing, Dept. JC 87, 103 Clover Green, Peachtree City, Georgia 30269.

May the blessings of God — the Father, Son and Holy Spirit, be with you as you search for a healthy life on earth and for everlasting peace.

Bibliography of References

Age Pages. National Institutes of Health. U.S. Department of Health and Human Services Publication. January 1984.

American Health. May 1984.

Arthritis Foundation. *Overcoming Rheumatoid Arthritis: What You Can Do For Yourself*. Arthritis Foundation. Atlanta, GA. 1983.

Bosco, Dominick. *Prevention*. Rodale Press. Emmasus, PA. July 1977.

Cawood, Frank W. *Vitamin Side Effects Revealed*. FC&A Publishing. Peachtree City, GA. 1986.

Cawood, Frank W. and Janice McCall Failes. *Hidden Health Secrets*. FC&A Publishing. Peachtree City, GA. 1986.

Cawood, Frank W., Rita Warmack, Janice McCall Failes and Gayle R. Cawood. *Arteries Cleaned Out Naturally: Scientific Facts and Fancies*. FC&A Publishing. Peachtree City, GA. 1986.

Changes ... Research on Aging and the Aged. National Institutes of Health.U.S. Department of Health and Human Services Publication. October 1980.

Failes, Janice M. editor. *Prescription Drug News*. FC&A Publishing. Peachtree City, GA. 1985.

Failes, Janice McCall and Frank W. Cawood. *Encyclopedia of Little Known Secrets of Perfect Natural Health*. FC&A Publishing. Peachtree City, GA. 1987.

Failes, Janice McCall and Frank W. Cawood. *Encyclopedia of Natural Health Secrets and Cures*. FC&A Publishing. Peachtree City, GA. 1988.

Failes, Janice McCall and Frank W. Cawood. *Natural Healing Encyclopedia*. FC&A Publishing. Peachtree City, GA. 1987.

Gershoff, Stanley N. Ph.d.., editor. *Tufts University Diet & Nutrition Letter*. Tufts University, New York, NY. 1985.

Kiely, Joseph M. M.D., editor. *Mayo Clinic Health Letter*. Mayo Clinic, Rochester, MN. 1984.

Insel, Paul M. Ph.D, editor. *Healthline*. San Carlos, CA. March 1985.

National Institute on Aging. National Institutes of Health. Publication No 83-1129. U.S. Department of Health and Human Services. July 1983.

National Enquirer. *Living With Arthritis*. Pocket Books. New York, NY. 1985.

Special Report on Aging 1983. National Institutes of Health. U.S. Department of Health and Human Services Publication. August 1983.

To Understand the Aging Process. National Institutes of Health. Publication No. 80-134. U.S. Department of Health and Human Services Publication. August 1980.

Weiner, Michael A. Ph.D. and Kathleen Goss. *Nutrition Against Aging*. Bantam Books, New York, NY. 1983.

"HE DIED WITH ARTERIES LIKE A BABY"

RESEARCHERS DISCOVER EVIDENCE THAT THE HUMAN BODY HAS ITS OWN NATURAL SYSTEM THAT HELPS KEEP THE ARTERIES CLEAN

(By Frank K. Wood)

Can your arteries be cleaned out naturally? That's what many doctors are asking themselves after an autopsy of a famous nutrition expert who committed suicide.

CAN THE BODY KEEP ITS ARTERIES CLEAN?

What interests the doctors is that the "free from artery disease" theory of the nutrition expert may be proven by his death! The doctor who performed the autopsy was, in his own words "amazed to find no evidence of coronary artery disease in a man of his age (69)". He said that the nutrition expert had "arteries like a baby". What's even more amazing is that the nutrition expert was diagnosed as actually having coronary artery disease 30 years earlier when he was 39 years old.

The nutrition expert put himself on a special program to fight coronary artery disease. You'll learn about it in a new $9.95 book for the general public, *"Arteries Cleaned Out Naturally"*.

It reveals a startling new discovery by medical researchers. They say they have discovered evidence that the human body has its own natural system that helps keep the arteries clean.

Case studies like this may be atypical. There is no proof that already narrowed or clogged arteries will open up when we start to do things which might help the body's natural cleansing process.

THE AMAZING STORY OF LDL's AND HDL's

You'll learn about the new scientific discovery that the human body seems to have its own natural system which helps keep the arteries clean.

You'll learn about how LDL molecules seem to carry cholesterol into the walls of coronary arteries and lead to heart and artery disease. You'll also learn about how other molecules, HDL's, seem to play a part in the body's natural cleansing system.

The recent discoveries about HDL's are important because researchers think that most coronary artery disease is avoidable. There's a lot we can do to help keep our arteries clean.

WHAT*"ARTERIES CLEANED OUT*

NATURALLY" REVEALS

- The amazing story of HDL's.
- The latest research evidence that the human body has its own natural system that helps keep the arteries clean.
- Four different types of heart and artery disease explained in easy-to-understand language.
- Why hardening of the arteries and high blood pressure may be higher now than years ago.
- Vitamins and minerals . . . can they help prevent artery disease?
- Exercise . . . one type that's harmful, another type that helps.
- Why some people get heart attacks even though they're health conscious.
- Heart surgery . . . when it's likely not to help . . . when relief may be obtained by other means.
- Why some fat people don't suffer from artery disease.
- Low-fat diets, are they helpful?
- Relaxation training . . . is it for you?
- Why foot problems are associated with high rates of heart attack.
- No-nonsense tips from researchers on artery cleansing.
- The smoking and heart disease connection.
- Does smoking really cause heart attacks?
- Does salt cause high blood pressure?
- How to add 10 years to your life.

IT'S EASY TO ORDER

Just return this notice with your name and address and a check for $9.95 plus $2.00 shipping and handling to our address: **FC&A, Dept. XOZ-2,** 103 Clover Green, Peachtree City, Georgia 30269. We will send you a copy of *"Arteries Cleaned Out Naturally"* right away.

Save! Return this notice with **$19.90** + $2.00 for two books. (No extra shipping and handling charges.)

You get a no-time-limit guarantee of satisfaction or your money back.

You must cut out and return this notice with your order. Copies will not be accepted!

IMPORTANT — FREE GIFT OFFER

All orders will receive a free gift. Order right away!

©PC&A 1988

"PRESCRIPTION DRUG KILLS DOCTOR"

TAGAMET® · MOTRIN® · TETRACYCLINE · INDERAL® · VALIUM® · TYLENOL/CODEINE

"Do you know the intended good effects and bad side effects of 783 prescription drugs ? Read this article for facts."

(By Frank K. Wood)

An Atlanta doctor has died from a freak drug reaction on a trip overseas. An infection he had didn't clear up after taking a drug so he took a different drug, too. The two drugs reacted with each other and caused crystallization in his kidneys. He had kidney failure and died a few days later.

WHAT YOUR DOCTOR DOESN'T TELL YOU ABOUT THE SIDE EFFECTS OF PRESCRIPTION DRUGS

This tragedy points to the fact that most doctors don't tell their patients about the side effects of the drugs they prescribe.

The reaction that killed the doctor and many other prescription drug side effects are clearly described in a new book, *"Prescription Drug Encyclopedia"* .

THE GOOD EFFECTS OF PRESCRIPTION DRUGS

You take drugs prescribed by your doctor for their good effects, like relieving pain, fighting infection, birth control, aiding sleep, calming down, fighting coughs, colds or allergies, or lowering heartbeat and blood pressure.

DO YOU HAVE ANY OF THESE BAD SIDE EFFECTS?

Prescription drugs can cause headache, upset stomach, constipation, stuffy nose, short breath, high blood pressure, fear and ringing sounds.

LATEST FACTS ON EACH DRUG

The book describes more than 783 of the most-often-used drugs. Facts are given in easy-to-understand words.

EASY TO READ

The book lists brand names, money-saving generic names, good effects, side effects, and warnings.

It explains drug categories. (For example: a drug may be called an "analgesic" . . . analgesic means "pain reliever").

Order this 30,000 word, easy-to-understand book explaining more than 783 drugs, edited by two pharmacists, right away.

IT'S EASY TO ORDER

Just return this notice with your name and address and a check for **$9.95** plus $2.00 shipping and handling to our following address: **FC&A, Dept. DOZ-2, 103 Clover Green, Peachtree City, Georgia, 30269.** We will send you a copy of *"Prescription Drug Encyclopedia"* right away.

Save! Return this notice with **$19.90 +** $2.00 for two books. (No extra shipping and handling charges.)

You get a no-time-limit guarantee of satisfaction or your money back.

You must cut out and return this notice with your order. Copies will not be accepted!

IMPORTANT— FREE GIFT OFFER

All orders will receive a free gift. Order right away!